CBEST Math Practice Workbook

2023

The Most Comprehensive Review for the Math Section of the CBEST Test

By

Reza Nazari

All inquiries should be addressed to:
info@effortlessMath.com
www.EffortlessMath.com

ISBN: 978-1-63719-147-7

Published by: **Effortless Math Education Inc.**

For Online Math Practice Visit www.EffortlessMath.com

#5 : Plugging In Numbers

"Plugging in numbers" is a strategy that can be applied to a wide range of different math problems on the CBEST Math test. This approach is typically used to simplify a challenging question so that it is more understandable. By using the strategy carefully, you can find the answer without too much trouble.

The concept is fairly straightforward–replace unknown variables in a problem with certain values. When selecting a number, consider the following:

- Choose a number that's basic (just not too basic). Generally, you should avoid choosing 1 (or even 0). A decent choice is 2.

- Try not to choose a number that is displayed in the problem.

- Make sure you keep your numbers different if you need to choose at least two of them.

- More often than not, choosing numbers merely lets you filter out some of your answer choices. As such, don't just go with the first choice that gives you the right answer.

- If several answers seem correct, then you'll need to choose another value and try again. This time, though, you'll just need to check choices that haven't been eliminated yet.

- If your question contains fractions, then a potential right answer may involve either an LCD (least common denominator) or an LCD multiple.

- 100 is the number you should choose when you are dealing with problems involving percentages.

CBEST Math – Test Day Tips

After practicing and reviewing all the math concepts you've been taught, and taking some CBEST mathematics practice tests, you'll be prepared for test day. Consider the following tips to be extra-ready come test time.

Before Your Test ··

What to do the night before:

■ **Relax!** One day before your test, study lightly or skip studying altogether. You shouldn't attempt to learn something new, either. There are plenty of reasons why studying the evening before a big test can work against you. Put it this way–a marathoner wouldn't go out for a sprint before the day of a big race. Mental marathoners–such as yourself–should not study for any more than one hour 24 hours before a CBEST test. That's because your brain requires some rest to be at its best. The night before your exam, spend some time with family or friends, or read a book.

■ **Avoid bright screens** - You'll have to get some good shuteye the night before your test. Bright screens (such as the ones coming from your laptop, TV, or mobile device) should be avoided altogether. Staring at such a screen will keep your brain up, making it hard to drift asleep at a reasonable hour.

■ **Make sure your dinner is healthy** - The meal that you have for dinner should be nutritious. Be sure to drink plenty of water as well. Load up on your complex carbohydrates, much like a marathon runner would do. Pasta, rice, and potatoes are ideal options here, as are vegetables and protein sources.

■ **Get your bag ready for test day** - The night prior to your test, pack your bag with your stationery, admissions pass, ID, and any other gear that you need. Keep the bag right by your front door.

■ **Make plans to reach the testing site** - Before going to sleep, ensure that you understand precisely how you will arrive at the site of the test. If parking is something you'll have to find first, plan for it. If you're dependent on public transit, then review the schedule. You should also make sure that the train/bus/subway/streetcar you use will be running. Find out about road closures as well. If a parent or friend is accompanying you, ensure that they understand what steps they have to take as well.

The Day of the Test

- **Get up reasonably early, but not too early.**

- **Have breakfast** - Breakfast improves your concentration, memory, and mood. As such, make sure the breakfast that you eat in the morning is healthy. The last thing you want to be is distracted by a grumbling tummy. If it's not your own stomach making those noises, another test taker close to you might be instead. Prevent discomfort or embarrassment by consuming a healthy breakfast. Bring a snack with you if you think you'll need it.

- **Follow your daily routine** - Do you watch Good Morning America each morning while getting ready for the day? Don't break your usual habits on the day of the test. Likewise, if coffee isn't something you drink in the morning, then don't take up the habit hours before your test. Routine consistency lets you concentrate on the main objective—doing the best you can on your test.

- **Wear layers** - Dress yourself up in comfortable layers. You should be ready for any kind of internal temperature. If it gets too warm during the test, take a layer off.

- **Get there on time** - The last thing you want to do is get to the test site late. Rather, you should be there 45 minutes prior to the start of the test. Upon your arrival, try not to hang out with anybody who is nervous. Any anxious energy they exhibit shouldn't influence you.

- **Leave the books at home** - No books should be brought to the test site. If you start developing anxiety before the test, books could encourage you to do some last-minute studying, which will only hinder you. Keep the books far away—better yet, leave them at home.

- **Make your voice heard** - If something is off, speak to a proctor. If medical attention is needed or if you'll require anything, consult the proctor prior to the start of the test. Any doubts you have should be clarified. You should be entering the test site with a state of mind that is completely clear.

■ **Have faith in yourself** - When you feel confident, you will be able to perform at your best. When you are waiting for the test to begin, envision yourself receiving an outstanding result. Try to see yourself as someone who knows all the answers, no matter what the questions are. A lot of athletes tend to use this technique—particularly before a big competition. Your expectations will be reflected by your performance.

During your test

■ **Be calm and breathe deeply** - You need to relax before the test, and some deep breathing will go a long way to help you do that. Be confident and calm. You got this. Everybody feels a little stressed out just before an evaluation of any kind is set to begin. Learn some effective breathing exercises. Spend a minute meditating before the test starts. Filter out any negative thoughts you have. Exhibit confidence when having such thoughts.

■ **Concentrate on the test** - Refrain from comparing yourself to anyone else. You shouldn't be distracted by the people near you or random noise. Concentrate exclusively on the test. If you find yourself irritated by surrounding noises, earplugs can be used to block sounds off close to you. Don't forget—the test is going to last several hours if you're taking more than one subject of the test. Some of that time will be dedicated to brief sections. Concentrate on the specific section you are working on during a particular moment. Do not let your mind wander off to upcoming or previous sections.

■ **Try to answer each question individually** - Focus only on the question you are working on. Use one of the test-taking strategies to solve the problem. If you aren't able to come up with an answer, don't get frustrated. Simply skip that question, then move onto the next one.

■ **Don't forget to breathe!** Whenever you notice your mind wandering, your stress levels boosting, or frustration brewing, take a thirty-second break. Shut your eyes, drop your pencil, breathe deeply, and let your shoulders relax. You will end up being more productive when you allow yourself to relax for a moment.

■ **Optimize your breaks** - When break time comes, use the restroom, have a snack, and reactivate your energy for the subsequent section. Doing some stretches can help stimulate your blood flow.

After your test

- **Take it easy** - You will need to set some time aside to relax and decompress once the test has concluded. There is no need to stress yourself out about what you could've said, or what you may have done wrong. At this point, there's nothing you can do about it. Your energy and time would be better spent on something that will bring you happiness for the remainder of your day.

- **Redoing the test** - Did you pass the test? Congratulations! Your hard work paid off!

  If you have failed your test, though, don't worry! The test can be retaken. In such cases, you will need to follow the retake policy. You also need to re-register to take the exam again.

Contents

Contents

Chapter 1: Fractions and Mixed Numbers

Math Topics that you'll learn in this Chapter:

- ✓ Simplifying Fractions
- ✓ Adding and Subtracting Fractions
- ✓ Multiplying and Dividing Fractions
- ✓ Adding Mixed Numbers
- ✓ Subtracting Mixed Numbers
- ✓ Multiplying Mixed Numbers
- ✓ Dividing Mixed Numbers

1

Simplifying Fractions

✎ *Simplify each fraction.*

1) $\dfrac{8}{16} =$

2) $\dfrac{7}{21} =$

3) $\dfrac{11}{44} =$

4) $\dfrac{6}{24} =$

5) $\dfrac{6}{18} =$

6) $\dfrac{18}{27} =$

7) $\dfrac{15}{55} =$

8) $\dfrac{24}{54} =$

9) $\dfrac{63}{72} =$

10) $\dfrac{40}{64} =$

11) $\dfrac{23}{46} =$

12) $\dfrac{35}{63} =$

13) $\dfrac{32}{36} =$

14) $\dfrac{81}{99} =$

15) $\dfrac{16}{64} =$

16) $\dfrac{14}{35} =$

17) $\dfrac{19}{38} =$

18) $\dfrac{18}{54} =$

19) $\dfrac{56}{70} =$

20) $\dfrac{40}{45} =$

21) $\dfrac{9}{90} =$

22) $\dfrac{20}{25} =$

23) $\dfrac{36}{42} =$

24) $\dfrac{40}{48} =$

25) $\dfrac{18}{54} =$

26) $\dfrac{48}{144} =$

Adding and Subtracting Fractions

✏️ *Calculate and write the answer in lowest term.*

1) $\frac{1}{3} + \frac{1}{5} =$

2) $\frac{2}{5} + \frac{3}{8} =$

3) $\frac{1}{3} - \frac{2}{9} =$

4) $\frac{4}{5} - \frac{2}{9} =$

5) $\frac{2}{9} + \frac{1}{3} =$

6) $\frac{3}{10} + \frac{2}{5} =$

7) $\frac{9}{10} - \frac{4}{5} =$

8) $\frac{7}{9} - \frac{3}{7} =$

9) $\frac{3}{4} + \frac{1}{3} =$

10) $\frac{3}{8} + \frac{2}{5} =$

11) $\frac{3}{4} - \frac{2}{5} =$

12) $\frac{7}{9} - \frac{2}{3} =$

13) $\frac{4}{9} + \frac{5}{6} =$

14) $\frac{2}{3} + \frac{1}{4} =$

15) $\frac{9}{10} - \frac{3}{5} =$

16) $\frac{7}{12} - \frac{1}{2} =$

17) $\frac{4}{5} + \frac{2}{3} =$

18) $\frac{5}{7} + \frac{1}{5} =$

19) $\frac{5}{9} - \frac{2}{5} =$

20) $\frac{3}{5} - \frac{2}{9} =$

21) $\frac{7}{9} + \frac{1}{7} =$

22) $\frac{5}{8} + \frac{2}{3} =$

23) $\frac{5}{7} - \frac{2}{5} =$

24) $\frac{7}{9} - \frac{3}{4} =$

25) $\frac{3}{5} - \frac{1}{6} =$

26) $\frac{3}{12} + \frac{2}{7} =$

Chapter 1: Fractions and Mixed Numbers

Multiplying and Dividing Fractions

✍ *Solve and write the answer in lowest term.*

1) $\frac{1}{3} \times \frac{9}{5} =$

2) $\frac{1}{4} \times \frac{3}{7} =$

3) $\frac{1}{5} \div \frac{1}{4} =$

4) $\frac{1}{6} \div \frac{5}{12} =$

5) $\frac{2}{3} \times \frac{4}{7} =$

6) $\frac{5}{7} \times \frac{3}{4} =$

7) $\frac{2}{5} \div \frac{3}{7} =$

8) $\frac{3}{7} \div \frac{5}{8} =$

9) $\frac{3}{8} \times \frac{4}{7} =$

10) $\frac{2}{9} \times \frac{6}{11} =$

11) $\frac{1}{10} \div \frac{3}{8} =$

12) $\frac{3}{10} \div \frac{4}{5} =$

13) $\frac{6}{7} \times \frac{4}{9} =$

14) $\frac{3}{7} \times \frac{5}{6} =$

15) $\frac{7}{9} \div \frac{6}{11} =$

16) $\frac{1}{15} \div \frac{2}{3} =$

17) $\frac{1}{13} \times \frac{1}{2} =$

18) $\frac{1}{12} \times \frac{4}{7} =$

19) $\frac{1}{15} \div \frac{4}{9} =$

20) $\frac{1}{16} \div \frac{1}{2} =$

21) $\frac{4}{7} \times \frac{5}{8} =$

22) $\frac{1}{11} \times \frac{4}{5} =$

23) $\frac{1}{16} \div \frac{5}{8} =$

24) $\frac{1}{15} \div \frac{2}{3} =$

25) $\frac{1}{13} \times \frac{2}{5} =$

26) $\frac{1}{18} \times \frac{3}{7} =$

4

Adding Mixed Numbers

✏️ *Solve and write the answer in lowest terms.*

1) $1\frac{1}{5} + 2\frac{2}{5} =$

2) $1\frac{1}{2} + 4\frac{5}{6} =$

3) $2\frac{4}{5} + 2\frac{3}{10} =$

4) $3\frac{1}{6} + 2\frac{2}{5} =$

5) $1\frac{5}{6} + 1\frac{2}{5} =$

6) $3\frac{5}{7} + 1\frac{2}{9} =$

7) $3\frac{5}{8} + 2\frac{1}{3} =$

8) $1\frac{6}{7} + 3\frac{2}{9} =$

9) $2\frac{5}{9} + 1\frac{1}{4} =$

10) $3\frac{7}{9} + 2\frac{5}{6} =$

11) $2\frac{1}{10} + 2\frac{2}{5} =$

12) $1\frac{3}{10} + 3\frac{4}{5} =$

13) $3\frac{1}{12} + 2\frac{1}{3} =$

14) $5\frac{1}{11} + 1\frac{1}{2} =$

15) $3\frac{1}{21} + 2\frac{2}{3} =$

16) $4\frac{1}{24} + 1\frac{5}{8} =$

17) $2\frac{1}{25} + 3\frac{3}{5} =$

18) $3\frac{1}{15} + 2\frac{2}{10} =$

19) $5\frac{6}{7} + 2\frac{1}{3} =$

20) $2\frac{1}{8} + 3\frac{3}{4} =$

21) $2\frac{5}{7} + 2\frac{2}{21} =$

22) $4\frac{1}{6} + 1\frac{4}{5} =$

23) $2\frac{1}{7} + 2\frac{3}{8} =$

24) $3\frac{1}{4} + 2\frac{2}{3} =$

25) $1\frac{1}{13} + 2\frac{3}{4} =$

26) $3\frac{2}{35} + 2\frac{5}{7} =$

Subtracting Mixed Numbers

✏️ *Solve and write the answer in lowest terms.*

1) $5\frac{2}{9} - 2\frac{1}{9} =$

2) $6\frac{2}{7} - 2\frac{1}{3} =$

3) $5\frac{3}{8} - 2\frac{3}{4} =$

4) $7\frac{2}{5} - 3\frac{1}{10} =$

5) $9\frac{5}{7} - 7\frac{4}{21} =$

6) $11\frac{7}{12} - 9\frac{5}{6} =$

7) $9\frac{5}{9} - 8\frac{1}{8} =$

8) $13\frac{7}{9} - 11\frac{3}{7} =$

9) $8\frac{7}{12} - 7\frac{3}{8} =$

10) $11\frac{5}{9} - 9\frac{1}{4} =$

11) $6\frac{5}{6} - 2\frac{2}{9} =$

12) $5\frac{7}{8} - 4\frac{1}{3} =$

13) $9\frac{5}{8} - 8\frac{1}{2} =$

14) $4\frac{9}{16} - 2\frac{1}{4} =$

15) $3\frac{2}{3} - 1\frac{2}{15} =$

16) $5\frac{1}{2} - 4\frac{2}{17} =$

17) $5\frac{6}{7} - 2\frac{1}{3} =$

18) $3\frac{3}{7} - 2\frac{2}{21} =$

19) $7\frac{3}{10} - 5\frac{2}{15} =$

20) $4\frac{5}{6} - 2\frac{2}{9} =$

21) $6\frac{3}{7} - 2\frac{2}{9} =$

22) $7\frac{4}{5} - 6\frac{3}{7} =$

23) $12\frac{3}{7} - 8\frac{1}{3} =$

24) $5\frac{4}{9} - 2\frac{5}{6} =$

25) $10\frac{1}{28} - 7\frac{3}{4} =$

26) $11\frac{5}{12} - 7\frac{5}{48} =$

Multiplying Mixed Numbers

✏️ *Solve and write the answer in lowest terms.*

1) $1\frac{1}{6} \times 1\frac{3}{7} =$

2) $5\frac{1}{6} \times 2\frac{1}{4} =$

3) $3\frac{3}{7} \times 1\frac{2}{9} =$

4) $3\frac{3}{8} \times 3\frac{1}{6} =$

5) $1\frac{1}{2} \times 5\frac{2}{3} =$

6) $3\frac{1}{2} \times 6\frac{2}{3} =$

7) $9\frac{1}{2} \times 2\frac{1}{6} =$

8) $2\frac{5}{8} \times 8\frac{3}{5} =$

9) $3\frac{4}{5} \times 4\frac{2}{3} =$

10) $5\frac{1}{3} \times 2\frac{2}{7} =$

11) $6\frac{1}{3} \times 3\frac{3}{4} =$

12) $7\frac{2}{3} \times 1\frac{8}{9} =$

13) $8\frac{1}{2} \times 2\frac{1}{6} =$

14) $4\frac{1}{5} \times 8\frac{2}{3} =$

15) $3\frac{1}{8} \times 5\frac{2}{3} =$

16) $2\frac{2}{7} \times 6\frac{2}{5} =$

17) $2\frac{3}{8} \times 7\frac{2}{3} =$

18) $1\frac{7}{8} \times 8\frac{2}{3} =$

19) $9\frac{1}{2} \times 3\frac{1}{5} =$

20) $2\frac{5}{8} \times 4\frac{1}{3} =$

21) $6\frac{1}{3} \times 3\frac{2}{5} =$

22) $5\frac{3}{4} \times 2\frac{2}{7} =$

23) $8\frac{1}{6} \times 2\frac{2}{7} =$

24) $4\frac{1}{6} \times 7\frac{1}{5} =$

25) $2\frac{1}{5} \times 2\frac{5}{8} =$

26) $6\frac{2}{3} \times 4\frac{3}{5} =$

Dividing Mixed Numbers

✎ *Solve and write the answer in lowest terms.*

1) $6\frac{1}{2} \div 4\frac{2}{5} =$

2) $1\frac{3}{8} \div 1\frac{1}{4} =$

3) $6\frac{2}{5} \div 2\frac{4}{5} =$

4) $7\frac{1}{3} \div 6\frac{3}{4} =$

5) $7\frac{2}{5} \div 3\frac{3}{4} =$

6) $2\frac{4}{5} \div 3\frac{2}{3} =$

7) $8\frac{3}{5} \div 4\frac{3}{4} =$

8) $6\frac{3}{4} \div 2\frac{2}{9} =$

9) $5\frac{2}{7} \div 2\frac{2}{9} =$

10) $2\frac{2}{5} \div 3\frac{3}{5} =$

11) $4\frac{3}{7} \div 1\frac{7}{8} =$

12) $2\frac{5}{7} \div 2\frac{4}{5} =$

13) $8\frac{3}{5} \div 6\frac{1}{5} =$

14) $2\frac{5}{8} \div 1\frac{8}{9} =$

15) $5\frac{6}{7} \div 2\frac{3}{4} =$

16) $1\frac{3}{5} \div 2\frac{3}{8} =$

17) $5\frac{3}{4} \div 3\frac{2}{5} =$

18) $2\frac{3}{4} \div 3\frac{1}{5} =$

19) $3\frac{2}{3} \div 1\frac{2}{5} =$

20) $4\frac{1}{4} \div 2\frac{2}{3} =$

21) $3\frac{5}{6} \div 2\frac{4}{5} =$

22) $2\frac{1}{8} \div 1\frac{3}{4} =$

23) $5\frac{1}{2} \div 4\frac{2}{5} =$

24) $6\frac{3}{7} \div 2\frac{1}{7} =$

25) $3\frac{3}{6} \div 1\frac{5}{7} =$

26) $4\frac{4}{9} \div 4\frac{2}{3} =$

Answers – Chapter 1

Simplifying Fractions

1) $\frac{1}{2}$

2) $\frac{1}{3}$

3) $\frac{1}{4}$

4) $\frac{1}{4}$

5) $\frac{1}{3}$

6) $\frac{2}{3}$

7) $\frac{3}{11}$

8) $\frac{4}{9}$

9) $\frac{7}{8}$

10) $\frac{5}{8}$

11) $\frac{1}{2}$

12) $\frac{5}{9}$

13) $\frac{8}{9}$

14) $\frac{9}{11}$

15) $\frac{1}{4}$

16) $\frac{2}{5}$

17) $\frac{1}{2}$

18) $\frac{1}{3}$

19) $\frac{4}{5}$

20) $\frac{8}{9}$

21) $\frac{1}{10}$

22) $\frac{4}{5}$

23) $\frac{6}{7}$

24) $\frac{5}{6}$

25) $\frac{1}{3}$

26) $\frac{1}{3}$

Adding and Subtracting Fractions

1) $\frac{8}{15}$

2) $\frac{31}{40}$

3) $\frac{1}{9}$

4) $\frac{26}{45}$

5) $\frac{5}{9}$

6) $\frac{7}{10}$

7) $\frac{1}{10}$

8) $\frac{22}{63}$

9) $\frac{13}{12}$

10) $\frac{31}{40}$

11) $\frac{7}{20}$

12) $\frac{1}{9}$

13) $\frac{23}{18}$

14) $\frac{11}{12}$

15) $\frac{3}{10}$

16) $\frac{1}{12}$

17) $\frac{22}{15}$

18) $\frac{32}{35}$

19) $\frac{7}{45}$

20) $\frac{17}{45}$

21) $\frac{58}{63}$

22) $\frac{31}{24}$

23) $\frac{11}{35}$

24) $\frac{1}{36}$

25) $\frac{13}{30}$

26) $\frac{15}{28}$

Multiplying and Dividing Fractions

1) $\frac{3}{5}$

2) $\frac{3}{28}$

3) $\frac{4}{5}$

4) $\frac{2}{5}$

5) $\frac{8}{21}$

6) $\frac{15}{28}$

7) $\frac{14}{15}$

8) $\frac{24}{35}$

9) $\frac{3}{14}$

10) $\frac{4}{33}$

11) $\frac{4}{15}$

12) $\frac{3}{8}$

13) $\frac{8}{21}$

14) $\frac{5}{14}$

15) $\frac{77}{54}$

16) $\frac{1}{10}$

17) $\frac{1}{26}$

18) $\frac{1}{21}$

19) $\frac{3}{20}$

20) $\frac{1}{8}$

21) $\frac{5}{14}$

22) $\frac{4}{55}$

23) $\frac{1}{10}$

24) $\frac{1}{10}$

25) $\frac{2}{65}$

26) $\frac{1}{42}$

Adding Mixed Numbers

1) $3\frac{3}{5}$

2) $6\frac{1}{3}$

3) $5\frac{1}{10}$

4) $5\frac{17}{30}$

5) $3\frac{7}{30}$

6) $4\frac{59}{63}$

7) $5\frac{23}{24}$

8) $5\frac{5}{63}$

9) $3\frac{29}{36}$

10) $6\frac{11}{18}$

11) $4\frac{1}{2}$

12) $5\frac{1}{10}$

13) $5\frac{5}{12}$

14) $6\frac{13}{22}$

15) $5\frac{5}{7}$

16) $5\frac{2}{3}$

17) $5\frac{16}{25}$

18) $5\frac{4}{15}$

19) $8\frac{4}{21}$

20) $5\frac{7}{8}$

21) $4\frac{17}{21}$

22) $5\frac{29}{30}$

23) $4\frac{29}{56}$

24) $5\frac{11}{12}$

25) $3\frac{43}{52}$

26) $5\frac{27}{35}$

Subtracting Mixed Numbers

1) $3\frac{1}{9}$

2) $3\frac{20}{21}$

3) $2\frac{5}{8}$

4) $4\frac{3}{10}$

5) $2\frac{11}{21}$

6) $1\frac{3}{4}$

7) $1\frac{31}{72}$

8) $2\frac{22}{63}$

9) $1\frac{5}{24}$

10) $2\frac{11}{36}$

11) $4\frac{11}{18}$

12) $1\frac{13}{24}$

13) $1\frac{1}{8}$

14) $2\frac{5}{16}$

15) $2\frac{8}{15}$

16) $1\frac{13}{34}$

17) $3\frac{11}{21}$

18) $1\frac{1}{3}$

19) $2\frac{1}{6}$

20) $2\frac{11}{18}$

21) $4\frac{13}{63}$

22) $1\frac{13}{35}$

23) $4\frac{2}{21}$

24) $2\frac{11}{18}$

25) $2\frac{2}{7}$

26) $4\frac{5}{16}$

Multiplying Mixed Numbers

1) $1\frac{2}{3}$

2) $11\frac{5}{8}$

3) $4\frac{4}{21}$

4) $10\frac{11}{16}$

5) $8\frac{1}{2}$

6) $23\frac{1}{3}$

7) $20\frac{7}{12}$

8) $22\frac{23}{40}$

9) $17\frac{11}{15}$

10) $12\frac{4}{21}$

11) $23\frac{3}{4}$

12) $14\frac{13}{27}$

13) $18\frac{5}{12}$

14) $36\frac{2}{5}$

15) $17\frac{17}{24}$

16) $14\frac{22}{35}$

17) $18\frac{5}{24}$

18) $16\frac{1}{4}$

19) $30\frac{2}{5}$

20) $11\frac{3}{8}$

21) $21\frac{8}{15}$

22) $13\frac{1}{7}$

23) $18\frac{2}{3}$

24) 30

25) $5\frac{31}{40}$

26) $30\frac{2}{3}$

Dividing Mixed Numbers

1) $1\frac{21}{44}$

2) $1\frac{1}{10}$

3) $2\frac{2}{7}$

4) $1\frac{7}{81}$

5) $1\frac{73}{75}$

6) $\frac{42}{55}$

7) $1\frac{77}{95}$

8) $3\frac{3}{80}$

9) $2\frac{53}{140}$

10) $\frac{2}{3}$

11) $2\frac{88}{105}$

12) $\frac{95}{98}$

13) $1\frac{12}{31}$

14) $1\frac{53}{136}$

15) $2\frac{10}{77}$

16) $\frac{64}{95}$

17) $1\frac{47}{68}$

18) $\frac{55}{64}$

19) $2\frac{13}{21}$

20) $1\frac{19}{32}$

21) $1\frac{31}{84}$

22) $1\frac{3}{14}$

23) $1\frac{1}{4}$

24) 3

25) $2\frac{1}{24}$

26) $\frac{20}{21}$

Chapter 2: Decimal

Math Topics that you'll learn in this Chapter:

- ✓ Comparing Decimals
- ✓ Rounding Decimals
- ✓ Adding and Subtracting Decimals
- ✓ Multiplying and Dividing Decimals

Chapter 2: Decimal

Comparing Decimals

✍ *Compare. Use* $>$*,* $=$*, and* $<$

1) 0.44 ☐ 0.044

2) 0.67 ☐ 0.68

3) 0.49 ☐ 0.79

4) 1.35 ☐ 1.45

5) 1.58 ☐ 1.75

6) 2.91 ☐ 2.85

7) 14.56 ☐ 1.456

8) 17.85 ☐ 17.89

9) 21.52 ☐ 21.052

10) 11.12 ☐ 11.03

11) 9.650 ☐ 9.65

12) 8.578 ☐ 8.568

13) 3.15 ☐ 0.315

14) 16.61 ☐ 16.16

15) 18.581 ☐ 8.991

16) 25.05 ☐ 2.505

17) 4.55 ☐ 4.65

18) 0.158 ☐ 1.58

19) 0.881 ☐ 0.871

20) 0.505 ☐ 0.510

21) 0.772 ☐ 0.777

22) 0.5 ☐ 0.500

23) 16.89 ☐ 15.89

24) 12.25 ☐ 12.35

25) 5.82 ☐ 5.69

26) 1.320 ☐ 1.032

27) 0.082 ☐ 0.088

28) 0.99 ☐ 0.099

29) 2.360 ☐ 2.840

30) 0.330 ☐ 0.303

31) 16.44 ☐ 1.664

32) 0.424 ☐ 0.442

Rounding Decimals

✎ *Round each number to the underlined place value.*

1) 3.960 =

2) 4.372 =

3) 11.136 =

4) 17.5 =

5) 1.981 =

6) 14.215 =

7) 17.548 =

8) 25.508 =

9) 31.089 =

10) 69.345 =

11) 9.457 =

12) 12.901 =

13) 2.658 =

14) 32.565 =

15) 6.058 =

16) 98.108 =

17) 27.705 =

18) 36.75 =

19) 9.08 =

20) 7.185 =

21) 22.547 =

22) 66.098 =

23) 87.75 =

24) 18.541 =

25) 10.258 =

26) 13.456 =

27) 71.084 =

28) 29.23 =

29) 43.45 =

30) 81.07 =

31) 92.366 =

32) 24.76 =

Adding and Subtracting Decimals

✍ *Solve.*

1) $11.62 + 18.23 =$

2) $13.78 + 16.58 =$

3) $56.30 - 45.68 =$

4) $59.36 - 30.88 =$

5) $24.32 + 26.45 =$

6) $36.25 + 18.37 =$

7) $47.85 - 35.12 =$

8) $85.65 - 67.48 =$

9) $25.49 + 34.18 =$

10) $19.99 + 48.66 =$

11) $46.32 - 27.77 =$

12) $54.62 - 48.12 =$

13) $24.42 + 16.54 =$

14) $52.13 + 12.32 =$

15) $82.36 - 78.65 =$

16) $64.12 - 49.15 =$

17) $36.41 + 24.52 =$

18) $85.96 - 74.63 =$

19) $52.62 - 42.54 =$

20) $21.20 + 24.58 =$

21) $32.15 + 17.17 =$

22) $96.32 - 85.54 =$

23) $89.78 - 69.85 =$

24) $29.28 + 39.79 =$

25) $11.11 + 19.99 =$

26) $28.82 + 20.88 =$

27) $63.14 - 28.91 =$

28) $56.61 - 49.72 =$

29) $66.14 + 32.12 =$

30) $30.19 + 25.83 =$

31) $68.21 - 25.10 =$

32) $76.57 - 45.13 =$

Multiplying and Dividing Decimals

✎ *Solve.*

1) $12.3 \times 0.2 =$

2) $12.6 \times 0.9 =$

3) $54.4 \div 2 =$

4) $64.8 \div 8 =$

5) $23.1 \times 0.3 =$

6) $1.2 \times 0.7 =$

7) $5.5 \div 0.5 =$

8) $64.8 \div 8 =$

9) $1.4 \times 0.5 =$

10) $4.5 \times 0.3 =$

11) $88.8 \div 4 =$

12) $10.5 \div 5 =$

13) $2.2 \times 0.3 =$

14) $0.2 \times 0.52 =$

15) $95.7 \div 100 =$

16) $36.6 \div 6 =$

17) $3.2 \times 2 =$

18) $4.1 \times 0.5 =$

19) $68.4 \div 2 =$

20) $27.9 \div 9 =$

21) $3.5 \times 4 =$

22) $4.8 \times 0.5 =$

23) $6.4 \div 4 =$

24) $72.8 \div 0.8 =$

25) $1.8 \times 3 =$

26) $6.5 \times 0.2 =$

27) $93.6 \div 3 =$

28) $45.15 \div 0.5 =$

29) $12.6 \times 0.5 =$

30) $13.2 \times 6 =$

31) $6.4 \div 0.8 =$

32) $98.6 \div 0.2 =$

Answers – Chapter 2

Comparing Decimals

1) $0.44 > 0.044$

2) $0.67 < 0.68$

3) $0.49 < 0.79$

4) $1.35 < 1.45$

5) $1.58 < 1.75$

6) $2.91 > 2.85$

7) $14.56 > 1.456$

8) $17.85 < 17.89$

9) $21.52 > 21.052$

10) $11.12 > 11.03$

11) $9.650 = 9.65$

12) $8.578 > 8.568$

13) $3.15 > 0.315$

14) $16.61 > 16.16$

15) $18.581 > 8.991$

16) $25.05 > 2.505$

17) $4.55 < 4.65$

18) $0.158 < 1.58$

19) $0.881 > 0.871$

20) $0.505 < 0.510$

21) $0.772 < 0.777$

22) $0.5 = 0.500$

23) $16.89 > 15.89$

24) $12.25 < 12.35$

25) $5.82 > 5.69$

26) $1.320 > 1.032$

27) $0.082 < 0.088$

28) $0.99 > 0.099$

29) $2.360 < 2.840$

30) $0.330 > 0.303$

31) $16.44 > 1.664$

32) $0.424 < 0.442$

Rounding Decimals

1) $\underline{3}.960 = 4$

2) $4.3\underline{72} = 4.37$

3) $11.1\underline{36} = 11.14$

4) $1\underline{7}.5 = 18$

5) $1.9\underline{81} = 1.98$

6) $14.\underline{2}15 = 14.2$

7) $17.5\underline{48} = 17.55$

8) $25.5\underline{08} = 25.51$

9) $3\underline{1}.089 = 31$

10) $69.\underline{3}45 = 69.3$

11) $9.4\underline{57} = 9.46$

12) $1\underline{2}.901 = 13$

13) $2.6\underline{58} = 2.66$

14) $32.\underline{5}65 = 32.6$

15) $6.0\underline{58} = 6.06$

16) $98.1\underline{08} = 98.11$

17) $27.\underline{7}05 = 27.7$

18) $3\underline{6}.75 = 37$

19) $9.\underline{0}8 = 9.1$

20) $7.\underline{1}85 = 7.2$

21) $22.5\underline{47} = 22.55$

22) $66.\underline{0}98 = 66.1$

23) $8\underline{7}.75 = 88$

24) $18.\underline{5}41 = 18.5$

25) $10.2\underline{58} = 10.26$

26) $13.\underline{4}56 = 13.5$

27) $71.0\underline{84} = 71.08$

28) $2\underline{9}.23 = 29$

29) $43.\underline{4}5 = 43.5$

30) $8\underline{1}.07 = 81$

31) $9\underline{2}.366 = 92$

32) $24.\underline{7}6 = 24.8$

Adding and Subtracting Decimals

1) 29.85	9) 59.67	17) 60.93	25) 31.1
2) 30.36	10) 68.65	18) 11.33	26) 49.7
3) 10.62	11) 18.55	19) 10.08	27) 34.23
4) 28.48	12) 6.5	20) 45.78	28) 6.89
5) 50.77	13) 40.96	21) 49.32	29) 98.26
6) 54.62	14) 64.45	22) 10.78	30) 56.02
7) 12.73	15) 3.71	23) 19.93	31) 43.11
8) 18.17	16) 14.97	24) 69.07	32) 31.44

Multiplying and Dividing Decimals

1) 2.46	9) 0.7	17) 6.4	25) 5.4
2) 11.34	10) 1.35	18) 2.05	26) 1.3
3) 27.2	11) 22.2	19) 34.2	27) 31.2
4) 8.1	12) 2.1	20) 3.1	28) 90.3
5) 6.93	13) 0.66	21) 14	29) 6.3
6) 0.84	14) 0.104	22) 2.4	30) 79.2
7) 11	15) 0.957	23) 1.6	31) 8
8) 8.1	16) 6.1	24) 91	32) 493

Chapter 3: Integers and Order of Operations

Math Topics that you'll learn in this Chapter:

- ✓ Adding and Subtracting Integers
- ✓ Multiplying and Dividing Integers
- ✓ Order of Operations
- ✓ Integers and Absolute Value

21

Chapter 3: Integers and Order of Operations

Adding and Subtracting Integers

✎ *Solve.*

1) $-(9) + 15 =$

2) $15 - (-11 - 9) =$

3) $(-10) + (-6) =$

4) $(-10) + (-6) + 7 =$

5) $-(23) + 19 =$

6) $(-7 + 5) - 9 =$

7) $28 + (-32) =$

8) $(-11) + (-9) + 5 =$

9) $25 - (8 - 7) =$

10) $-(29) + 17 =$

11) $(-38) + (-3) + 29 =$

12) $15 - (-7 + 9) =$

13) $24 - (8 - 2) =$

14) $(-7 + 4) - 9 =$

15) $(-17) + (-3) + 9 =$

16) $(-26) + (-7) + 8 =$

17) $(-9) + (-11) =$

18) $8 - (-23 - 13) =$

19) $(-16) + (-2) =$

20) $25 - (7 - 4) =$

21) $23 + (-12) =$

22) $(-18) + (-6) =$

23) $17 - (-21 - 7) =$

24) $-(28) - (-16) + 5 =$

25) $(-9 + 4) - 8 =$

26) $(-28) + (-6) + 17 =$

27) $-(21) - (-15) + 9 =$

28) $(-31) + (-6) =$

29) $(-18) + (-10) + 13 =$

30) $(-30) + (-11) + 12 =$

31) $-(28) - (-10) + 6 =$

32) $6 - (-16 - 11) =$

Multiplying and Dividing Integers

✎ **Solve.**

1) $(-6) \times (-7) =$

2) $8 \times (-5) =$

3) $48 \div (-8) =$

4) $(-72) \div 9 =$

5) $(4) \times (-6) =$

6) $(-9) \times (-11) =$

7) $(10) \div (-5) =$

8) $144 \div (-12) =$

9) $(10) \times (-2) =$

10) $(-8) \times (-2) \times 5 =$

11) $(8) \div (-2) =$

12) $45 \div (-15) =$

13) $(5) \times (-7) =$

14) $(-6) \times (-5) \times 4 =$

15) $(12) \div (-6) =$

16) $(14) \div (-7) =$

17) $196 \div (-14) =$

18) $(27 - 13) \times (-2) =$

19) $125 \div (-5) =$

20) $66 \div (-6) =$

21) $(-6) \times (-5) \times 3 =$

22) $(15 - 6) \times (-3) =$

23) $(32 - 24) \div (-4) =$

24) $72 \div (-6) =$

25) $(-14 + 8) \times (-7) =$

26) $(-3) \times (-9) \times 3 =$

27) $84 \div (-12) =$

28) $(-12) \times (-10) =$

29) $22 \times (-3) =$

30) $(-2) \times (-6) \times 5 =$

31) $(24) \div (-3) =$

32) $(-15) \div (3) =$

Order of Operation

✎ *Calculate.*

1) $16 + (30 \div 5) =$

2) $(3 \times 9) \div (-3) =$

3) $57 - (3 \times 8) =$

4) $(-12) \times (7 - 3) =$

5) $(18 - 7) \times (6) =$

6) $(6 \times 10) \div (12 + 3) =$

7) $(13 \times 2) - (24 \div 6) =$

8) $(-5) + (4 \times 3) + 8 =$

9) $(4 \times 2^3) + (16 - 9) =$

10) $(3^2 \times 7) \div (-2 + 1) =$

11) $[-2(48 \div 2^3)] - 6 =$

12) $(-4) + (7 \times 8) + 18 =$

13) $(3 \times 7) + (16 - 7) =$

14) $[3^3 \times (48 \div 2^3)] \div (-2) =$

15) $(14 \times 3) - (3^4 \div 9) =$

16) $(96 \div 12) \times (-3) =$

17) $(48 \div 2^2) \times (-2) =$

18) $(56 \div 7) \times (-5) =$

19) $(-2^2) + (7 \times 9) - 21 =$

20) $(2^4 - 9) \times (-6) =$

21) $[4^3 \times (50 \div 5^2)] \div (-16) =$

22) $(3^2 \times 4^2) \div (-4 + 2) =$

23) $6^2 - (-6 \times 4) + 3 =$

24) $4^2 - (5^2 \times 3) =$

25) $(-4) + (12^2 \div 3^2) - 7^2 =$

26) $(3^2 \times 5) + (-5^2 - 9) =$

27) $2[(3^2 \times 5) \times (-6)] =$

28) $(11^2 - 2^2) - (-7^2) =$

29) $(2^2 \times 5) - (64 \div 8) =$

30) $2[(3^2 \times 4) + (35 \div 5)] =$

31) $(4^2 \times 3) \div (-6) =$

32) $3^2[(4^3 \div 16) - (3^3 \div 27)] =$

Integers and Absolute Value

✎ *Calculate.*

1) $4 - |6 - 10| =$

2) $|14| - \dfrac{|-18|}{3} =$

3) $\dfrac{|8 \times -8|}{4} \times \dfrac{|-20|}{5} =$

4) $|12 \times 3| + \dfrac{|-81|}{9} =$

5) $4 - |11 - 18| - |3| =$

6) $|18| - \dfrac{|-12|}{4} =$

7) $\dfrac{|5 \times -8|}{10} \times \dfrac{|-22|}{11} =$

8) $|9 \times 3| + \dfrac{|-36|}{4} =$

9) $|-42 + 7| \times \dfrac{|-2 \times 5|}{10} =$

10) $6 - |17 - 11| - |5| =$

11) $|13| - \dfrac{|-54|}{6} =$

12) $\dfrac{|9 \times -4|}{12} \times \dfrac{|-45|}{9} =$

13) $|-75 + 50| \times \dfrac{|-4 \times 5|}{5} =$

14) $\dfrac{|-26|}{13} \times \dfrac{|-32|}{8} =$

15) $14 - |8 - 18| - |-12| =$

16) $|29| - \dfrac{|-20|}{5} =$

17) $\dfrac{|3 \times 8|}{2} \times \dfrac{|-33|}{3} =$

18) $|-45 + 15| \times \dfrac{|-12 \times 5|}{6} =$

19) $\dfrac{|-50|}{5} \times \dfrac{|-77|}{11} =$

20) $12 - |2 - 7| - |15| =$

21) $|18| - \dfrac{|-45|}{15} =$

22) $\dfrac{|7 \times 8|}{4} \times \dfrac{|-48|}{12} =$

23) $\dfrac{|30 \times 2|}{3} \times |-12| =$

24) $\dfrac{|-36|}{9} \times \dfrac{|-80|}{8} =$

25) $|-30 + 9| \times \dfrac{|-8 \times 5|}{8} =$

26) $|16| - \dfrac{|-18|}{3} =$

27) $12 - |10 - 24| + |5| =$

28) $|-38 + 8| \times \dfrac{|-5 \times 6|}{10} =$

Answers – Chapter 3

Adding and Subtracting Integers

1) 6	9) 24	17) −20	25) −13
2) 35	10) −12	18) 44	26) −17
3) −16	11) −12	19) −18	27) 3
4) −9	12) 13	20) 22	28) −37
5) −4	13) 18	21) 11	29) −15
6) −11	14) −12	22) −24	30) −29
7) −4	15) −11	23) 45	31) −12
8) −15	16) −25	24) −7	32) 33

Multiplying and Dividing Integers

1) 42	9) −20	17) −14	25) 42
2) −40	10) 80	18) −28	26) 81
3) −6	11) −4	19) −25	27) −7
4) −8	12) −3	20) −11	28) 120
5) −24	13) −35	21) 90	29) −66
6) 99	14) 120	22) −27	30) 60
7) −2	15) −2	23) −2	31) −8
8) −12	16) −2	24) −12	32) −5

Order of Operation

1) 22	9) 39	17) −24	25) −37
2) −9	10) −63	18) −40	26) 11
3) 33	11) −18	19) 38	27) −540
4) −48	12) 70	20) −42	28) 166
5) 66	13) 30	21) −8	29) 12
6) 4	14) −81	22) −72	30) 86
7) 22	15) 33	23) 63	31) −8
8) 15	16) −24	24) −59	32) 27

Integers and Absolute Value

1) 0	8) 36	15) −8	22) 56
2) 8	9) 35	16) 25	23) 240
3) 64	10) −5	17) 132	24) 40
4) 45	11) 4	18) 300	25) 105
5) −6	12) 15	19) 70	26) 10
6) 15	13) 100	20) −8	27) 3
7) 8	14) 8	21) 15	28) 90

Chapter 4: Ratios and Proportions

Math Topics that you'll learn in this Chapter:

- ✓ Simplifying Ratios
- ✓ Proportional Ratios
- ✓ Similarity and Ratios
- ✓ Simple Interest

Simplifying Ratios

✍ *Simplify each ratio.*

1) $3:21 = $ ___ : ___

2) $4:16 = $ ___ : ___

3) $\frac{2}{28} = -$

4) $\frac{18}{45} = -$

5) $10:30 = $ ___ : ___

6) $5:30 = $ ___ : ___

7) $\frac{34}{38} = -$

8) $\frac{45}{63} = -$

9) $10:45 = $ ___ : ___

10) $20:30 = $ ___ : ___

11) $\frac{40}{64} = -$

12) $\frac{10}{110} = -$

13) $8:12 = $ ___ : ___

14) $16:20 = $ ___ : ___

15) $\frac{24}{48} = -$

16) $\frac{21}{77} = -$

17) $8:24 = $ ___ : ___

18) $9 \text{ to } 36 = $ ___ : ___

19) $\frac{64}{72} = -$

20) $\frac{45}{60} = -$

21) $12:15 = $ ___ : ___

22) $18:54 = $ ___ : ___

23) $\frac{36}{54} = -$

24) $\frac{48}{104} = -$

25) $12:48 = $ ___ : ___

26) $18:72 = $ ___ : ___

27) $\frac{15}{75} = -$

28) $\frac{46}{52} = -$

Proportional Ratios

✎ *Solve each proportion for* x.

1) $\frac{4}{7} = \frac{8}{x}$, $x =$ ____

2) $\frac{9}{12} = \frac{x}{8}$, $x =$ ____

3) $\frac{3}{5} = \frac{12}{x}$, $x =$ ____

4) $\frac{3}{10} = \frac{x}{50}$, $x =$ ____

5) $\frac{3}{11} = \frac{15}{x}$, $x =$ ____

6) $\frac{6}{15} = \frac{x}{45}$, $x =$ ____

7) $\frac{6}{19} = \frac{12}{x}$, $x =$ ____

8) $\frac{7}{16} = \frac{x}{32}$, $x =$ ____

9) $\frac{18}{21} = \frac{54}{x}$, $x =$ ____

10) $\frac{13}{15} = \frac{39}{x}$, $x =$ ____

11) $\frac{9}{13} = \frac{72}{x}$, $x =$ ____

12) $\frac{8}{30} = \frac{x}{180}$, $x =$ ____

13) $\frac{3}{19} = \frac{9}{x}$, $x =$ ____

14) $\frac{1}{3} = \frac{x}{90}$, $x =$ ____

15) $\frac{25}{45} = \frac{x}{9}$, $x =$ ____

16) $\frac{1}{6} = \frac{9}{x}$, $x =$ ____

17) $\frac{7}{9} = \frac{63}{x}$, $x =$ ____

18) $\frac{54}{72} = \frac{x}{8}$, $x =$ ____

19) $\frac{32}{40} = \frac{4}{x}$, $x =$ ____

20) $\frac{21}{42} = \frac{x}{6}$, $x =$ ____

21) $\frac{56}{72} = \frac{7}{x}$, $x =$ ____

22) $\frac{1}{14} = \frac{x}{42}$, $x =$ ____

23) $\frac{5}{7} = \frac{75}{x}$, $x =$ ____

24) $\frac{30}{48} = \frac{x}{8}$, $x =$ ____

25) $\frac{36}{88} = \frac{9}{x}$, $x =$ ____

26) $\frac{62}{68} = \frac{x}{34}$, $x =$ ____

27) $\frac{42}{60} = \frac{x}{10}$, $x =$ ____

28) $\frac{8}{9} = \frac{x}{108}$, $x =$ ____

29) $\frac{40}{6} = \frac{x}{3}$, $x =$ ____

30) $\frac{88}{121} = \frac{x}{11}$, $x =$ ____

31) $\frac{10}{24} = \frac{x}{48}$, $x =$ ____

32) $\frac{32}{80} = \frac{x}{10}$, $x =$ ____

Create Proportion

✏️ *State if each pair of ratios form a proportion.*

1) $\frac{3}{8}$ and $\frac{24}{50}$

2) $\frac{3}{11}$ and $\frac{6}{22}$

3) $\frac{4}{5}$ and $\frac{16}{20}$

4) $\frac{5}{11}$ and $\frac{12}{33}$

5) $\frac{5}{10}$ and $\frac{15}{30}$

6) $\frac{4}{13}$ and $\frac{8}{24}$

7) $\frac{6}{9}$ and $\frac{24}{36}$

8) $\frac{7}{12}$ and $\frac{14}{20}$

9) $\frac{3}{8}$ and $\frac{27}{72}$

10) $\frac{12}{20}$ and $\frac{36}{60}$

11) $\frac{11}{12}$ and $\frac{55}{60}$

12) $\frac{12}{15}$ and $\frac{24}{25}$

13) $\frac{15}{19}$ and $\frac{20}{38}$

14) $\frac{10}{14}$ and $\frac{40}{56}$

15) $\frac{11}{13}$ and $\frac{44}{39}$

16) $\frac{15}{16}$ and $\frac{30}{32}$

17) $\frac{17}{19}$ and $\frac{34}{48}$

18) $\frac{5}{18}$ and $\frac{15}{54}$

19) $\frac{3}{14}$ and $\frac{18}{42}$

20) $\frac{7}{11}$ and $\frac{14}{32}$

21) $\frac{8}{11}$ and $\frac{32}{44}$

22) $\frac{8}{14}$ and $\frac{24}{54}$

✏️ *Solve.*

23) The ratio of boys to girls in a class is 3: 4. If there are 27 boys in the class, how many girls are in that class? _____

24) The ratio of red marbles to blue marbles in a bag is 5: 6. If there are 66 marbles in the bag, how many of the marbles are red? _____

25) You can buy 6 cans of green beans at a supermarket for $3.60. How much does it cost to buy 48 cans of green beans? _____

Similarity and Ratios

✎ *Each pair of figures is similar. Find the missing side.*

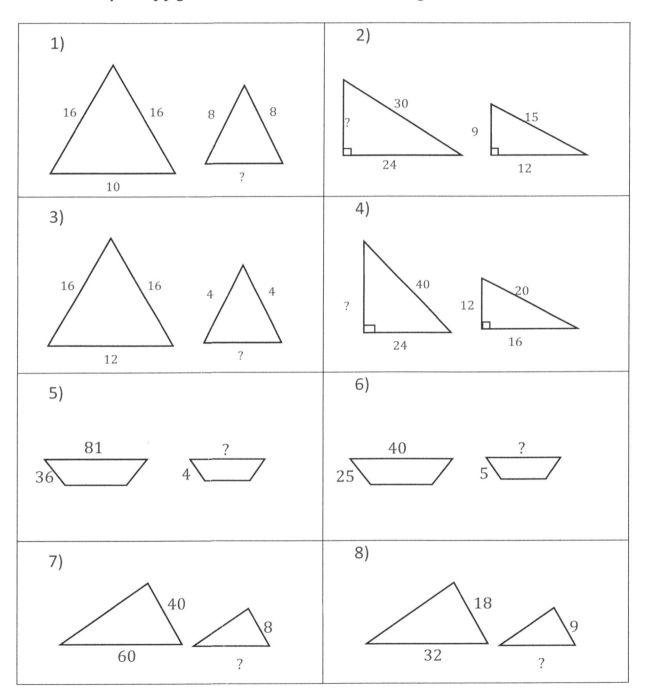

1)

16   16

8   8

10   ?

2)

30

?

24   9   15

12

3)

16   16

12   4   4

?

4)

40

?   12   20

24   16

5)

81   ?

36   4

6)

40   ?

25   5

7)

40

60   8

?

8)

18

32   9

?

Simple Interest

✍ *Determine the simple interest for these loans.*

1) $400 at 6% for 4 years. $__

2) $580 at 3.5% for 5 years. $_

3) $320 at 4% for 6 years. $__

4) $510 at 8% for 3 years. $__

5) $690 at 5% for 6 months. $__

6) $620 at 7% for 3 years. $__

7) $650 at 4.5% for 10 years. $__

8) $850 at 4% for 2 years. $__

9) $640 at 7% for 3 years. $__

10) $300 at 9% for 9 months. $__

11) $760 at 8% for 2 years. $_

12) $910 at 5% for 5 years. $__

13) $540 at 3% for 6 years. $__

14) $780 at 2.5% for 4 years. $__

15) $1,600 at 7% for 3 months. $__

16) $310 at 4% for 4 years. $__

17) $950 at 6% for 5 years. $__

18) $280 at 8% for 7 years. $__

19) $310 at 6% for 3 years. $__

20) $990 at 5% for 4 months. $__

21) $380 at 6% for 5 years. $__

22) $580 at 6% for 4 years. $__

23) $1,200 at 4% for 5 years. $__

24) $3,100 at 5% for 6 years. $__

25) $5,200 at 8% for 2 years. $__

26) $1,400 at 4% for 3 years. $__

27) $300 at 3% for 8 months. $__

28) $150 at 3.5% for 4 years. $__

29) $170 at 6% for 2 years. $__

30) $940 at 8% for 5 years. $__

31) $960 at 1.5% for 8 years. $_

32) $240 at 5% for 4 months. $__

33) $280 at 2% for 5 years. $__

34) $880 at 3% for 2 years. $__

35) $2,200 at 4.5% for 2 years. $__

36) $2,400 at 7% for 3 years. $__

37) $1,800 at 5% for 6 months. $__

38) $190 at 4% for 2 years. $__

39) $480 at 6% for 5 years. $__

40) $700 at 5% for 6 years. $_

Answers – Chapter 4

Simplifying Ratios

1) $1:7$

2) $1:4$

3) $\frac{1}{14}$

4) $\frac{2}{5}$

5) $1:3$

6) $1:6$

7) $\frac{17}{19}$

8) $\frac{5}{7}$

9) $2:9$

10) $2:3$

11) $\frac{5}{8}$

12) $\frac{1}{11}$

13) $2:3$

14) $4:5$

15) $\frac{1}{2}$

16) $\frac{3}{11}$

17) $1:3$

18) 1 to 4

19) $\frac{8}{9}$

20) $\frac{3}{4}$

21) $4:5$

22) $1:3$

23) $\frac{2}{3}$

24) $\frac{6}{13}$

25) $1:4$

26) $1:4$

27) $\frac{1}{5}$

28) $\frac{23}{26}$

Proportional Ratios

1) $x = 14$

2) $x = 6$

3) $x = 20$

4) $x = 15$

5) $x = 55$

6) $x = 18$

7) $x = 38$

8) $x = 14$

9) $x = 63$

10) $x = 45$

11) $x = 104$

12) $x = 48$

13) $x = 57$

14) $x = 30$

15) $x = 5$

16) $x = 54$

17) $x = 81$

18) $x = 6$

19) $x = 5$

20) $x = 3$

21) $x = 9$

22) $x = 3$

23) $x = 105$

24) $x = 5$

25) $x = 22$

26) $x = 31$

27) $x = 7$

28) $x = 96$

29) $x = 20$

30) $x = 8$

31) $x = 20$

32) $x = 4$

Create Proportion

1) *No*	10) *Yes*	19) *No*
2) *Yes*	11) *Yes*	20) *No*
3) *Yes*	12) *No*	21) *Yes*
4) *No*	13) *No*	22) *No*
5) *Yes*	14) *Yes*	23) 36 *girls*
6) *No*	15) *No*	24) 30 *red marbles*
7) *Yes*	16) *Yes*	25) $28.80
8) *No*	17) *No*	
9) *Yes*	18) *Yes*	

Similarity and Ratios

1) 5	5) 9
2) 18	6) 8
3) 3	7) 12
4) 32	8) 16

Simple Interest

1) $96	15) $28	29) $20.40
2) $101.50	16) $49.60	30) $376
3) $76.80	17) $285	31) $115.20
4) $122.40	18) $156.80	32) $4
5) $17.25	19) $55.80	33) $28
6) $130.20	20) $16.5	34) $52.80
7) $292.50	21) $114	35) $198
8) $68	22) $139.20	36) $504
9) $134.40	23) $240	37) $45
10) $20.25	24) $930	38) $15.20
11) $121.60	25) $832	39) $144
12) $227.50	26) $168	40) $210
13) $97.20	27) $6	
14) $78	28) $21	

Chapter 5:
Percentage

Math Topics that you'll learn in this Chapter:

- ✓ Percent Problems
- ✓ Percent of Increase and Decrease
- ✓ Discount, Tax and Tip

39

Percent Problems

✏ Solve each problem.

1) What is 4 percent of 280? ____

2) What is 25 percent of 500? ____

3) What is 10 percent of 460? ____

4) What is 34 percent of 260? ____

5) What is 60 percent of 850? ____

6) 63 is what percent of 300? ____%

7) 80 is what percent of 400? ____%

8) 70 is what percent of 700? ____%

9) 84 is what percent of 600? ___%

10) 90 is what percent of 300? ___%

11) 24 is what percent of 150? ___%

12) 12 is what percent of 80? ____%

13) 4 is what percent of 50? ____%

14) 110 is what percent of 500? _%

15) 16 is what percent of 400? __%

16) 39 is what percent of 300? ___%

17) 56 is what percent of 200? ___%

18) 30 is what percent of 500? ___%

19) 84 is what percent of 700? ___%

20) 40 is what percent of 500? __%

21) 26 is what percent of 100? __ %

22) 45 is what percent of 900? __%

23) 60 is what percent of 400? ___%

24) 18 is what percent of 900? ___%

25) 75 is what percent of 250? ___%

26) 27 is what percent of 900? ___%

27) 49 is what percent of 700? ___%

28) 81 is what percent of 900? ___%

29) 90 is what percent of 500? ___%

30) 82 is what percent of 410? ___%

31) 14 is 35 percent of what number? ____

32) 90 is 6 percent of what number? ____

33) 80 is 40 percent of what number? ____

34) 80 is 20 percent of what number? ____

35) 30 is 6 percent of what number? ____

36) 64 is 8 percent of what number? ____

Chapter 5: Percentage

Percent of Increase and Decrease

✎ *Solve each percent of change word problem.*

1) Bob got a raise, and his hourly wage increased from $30 to $42. What is the percent increase? _____ %

2) The price of gasoline rose from $4.40 to $4.62 in one month. By what percent did the gas price rise? _____ %

3) In a class, the number of students has been increased from 25 to 32. What is the percent increase? _____ %

4) The price of a pair of shoes increases from $24 to $30. What is the percent increase? ____ %

5) In a class, the number of students has been decreased from 24 to 18. What is the percentage decrease? _____ %

6) Nick got a raise, and his hourly wage increased from $50 to $55. What is the percent increase? _____ %

7) A coat was originally priced at $60. It went on sale for $54. What was the percent that the coat was discounted? _____ %

8) The price of a pair of shoes increases from $12 to $18. What is the percent increase? ____ %

9) A house was purchased in 2002 for $150,000. It is now valued at $132,000. What is the rate (percent) of depreciation for the house?_____ %

10) The price of gasoline rose from $4.00 to $4.20 in one month. By what percent did the gas price rise? _____ %

Chapter 5: Percentage

Discount, Tax and Tip

✍ *Find the missing values.*

1) Original price of a computer: $540, Tax: 6%, Selling price: $_____

2) Original price of a sofa: $400, Tax: 14%, Selling price: $_____

3) Original price of a table: $560, Tax: 15%, Selling price: $_____

4) Original price of a cell phone: $740, Tax: 24%, Selling price: $_____

5) Original price of a printer: $400, Tax: 22%, Selling price: $_____

6) Original price of a computer: $600, Tax: 15%, Selling price: $_____

7) Restaurant bill: $24.00, Tip: 25%, Final amount: $_____

8) Original price of a cell phone: $300 Tax: 8%, Selling price: $_____

9) Original price of a carpet: $800, Tax: 25%, Selling price: $_____

10) Original price of a camera: $200 Discount: 35%, Selling price: $_____

11) Original price of a dress: $560 Discount: 10%, Selling price: $___

12) Original price of a monitor: $420 Discount: 6%, Selling price: $____

13) Original price of a laptop: $880 Discount: 16%, Selling price: $____

14) Restaurant bill: $64.00, Tip: 20%, Final amount: $____

Answers – Chapter 5

Percent Problems

1) 11.2	13) 8%	25) 30%
2) 125	14) 22%	26) 3%
3) 46	15) 4%	27) 7%
4) 88.4	16) 13%	28) 9%
5) 510	17) 28%	29) 18%
6) 21%	18) 6%	30) 20%
7) 20%	19) 12%	31) 40
8) 10%	20) 8%	32) 1,500
9) 14%	21) 26%	33) 200
10) 30%	22) 5%	34) 400
11) 16%	23) 15%	35) 500
12) 15%	24) 2%	36) 800

Percent of Increase and Decrease

1) 40%	5) 25%	9) 12%
2) 5%	6) 10%	10) 5%
3) 28%	7) 10%	
4) 25%	8) 50%	

Discount, Tax and Tip

1) $572.40

2) $456

3) $644

4) $917.60

5) $488

6) $690

7) $30.00

8) $324

9) $1,000

10) $130

11) $504

12) $394.8

13) $739.2

14) $76.80

Chapter 6:
Expressions and Variables

Math Topics that you'll learn in this Chapter:

- ✓ Simplifying Variable Expressions
- ✓ Simplifying Polynomial Expressions
- ✓ Evaluating One Variable
- ✓ Evaluating Two Variables
- ✓ The Distributive Property

Simplifying Variable Expressions

✍ *Simplify and write the answer.*

1) $6x + 2 + 3x =$

2) $7x + 4 - 6x =$

3) $-1 - x^2 - 9x^2 =$

4) $(-5)(6x - 2) =$

5) $3 + 10x^2 + 2x =$

6) $8x^2 + 6x + 7x^2 =$

7) $2x^2 - 5x - 7x =$

8) $x - 3 + 5 - 3x =$

9) $2 - 3x + 12 - 2x =$

10) $5x^2 - 12x^2 + 8x =$

11) $2x^2 + 6x + 3x^2 =$

12) $2x^2 - 2x - x =$

13) $2x^2 - (-8x + 6) =$

14) $4x + 6(2 - 5x) =$

15) $10x + 8(10x - 6) =$

16) $9(-2x - 6) - 5 =$

17) $32x - 4 + 23 + 2x =$

18) $8x - 12x - x^2 + 13 =$

19) $(-6)(8x - 4) + 10x =$

20) $14x - 5(5 - 8x) =$

21) $23x + 4(9x + 3) + 12 =$

22) $3(-7x + 5) + 20x =$

23) $12x - 3x(x + 9) =$

24) $7x + 5x(3 - 3x) =$

25) $5x(-8x + 12) + 14x =$

26) $40x + 12 + 2x^2 =$

27) $5x(x - 3) - 10 =$

28) $8x - 7 + 8x + 2x^2 =$

29) $6x - 2x^2 - 6x^2 - 5 =$

30) $3 + x^2 - 4x^2 - 10x =$

31) $10x + 6x^2 + 5x + 18 =$

32) $20 + 12x^2 + 7x - 6x^2 =$

Simplifying Polynomial Expressions

✎ *Simplify and write the answer.*

1) $(3x^3 + 4x^2) - (10x + 3x^2) = $ _____

2) $(-4x^5 + 4x^3) - (6x^3 + 5x^2) = $ _____

3) $(10x^4 + 6x^2) - (x^2 - 8x^4) = $ _____

4) $6x - 2x^2 - 3(2x^2 + 5x^3) = $ _____

5) $(2x^3 - 3) + 3(2x^2 - 3x^3) = $ _____

6) $4(4x^3 - 2x) - (3x^3 - 2x^4) = $ _____

7) $2(4x - 3x^3) - 3(3x^3 + 4x^2) = $ _____

8) $(2x^2 - 2x) - (2x^3 + 5x^2) = $ _____

9) $2x^3 - (4x^4 + 2x) + x^2 = $ _____

10) $x^4 - 9(x^2 + x) - 5x = $ _____

11) $(-2x^2 - x^4) + (4x^4 - x^2) = $ _____

12) $4x^2 - 5x^3 + 15x^4 - 12x^3 = $ _____

13) $3x^2 - 2x^4 + 12x^4 - 10x^3 = $ _____

14) $4x^2 + 6x^3 - 8x^2 + 14x = $ _____

15) $3x^4 - 6x^5 + 7x^4 - 9x^2 = $ _____

16) $5x^3 + 15x - 4x^2 - 3x^3 = $ _____

Chapter 6: Expressions and Variables

Evaluating One Variable

✍ *Evaluate each expression using the value given.*

1) $x = 2 \Rightarrow 5x - 10 =$

2) $x = 3 \Rightarrow 6x - 12 =$

3) $x = 4 \Rightarrow 6x + 8 =$

4) $x = 6 \Rightarrow 2x + 4 =$

5) $x = 4 \Rightarrow 4x - 8 =$

6) $x = 2 \Rightarrow 5x - 2x + 10 =$

7) $x = 3 \Rightarrow 2x - x - 6 =$

8) $x = 4 \Rightarrow 6x - 3x + 4 =$

9) $x = -2 \Rightarrow 4x - 6x - 5 =$

10) $x = -1 \Rightarrow 3x - 5x + 11 =$

11) $x = 1 \Rightarrow x - 7x + 12 =$

12) $x = 2 \Rightarrow 2(-3x + 4) =$

13) $x = 3 \Rightarrow 4(-5x - 2) =$

14) $x = 2 \Rightarrow 5(-2x - 4) =$

15) $x = -2 \Rightarrow 3(-4x - 5) =$

16) $x = 3 \Rightarrow 8x + 5 =$

17) $x = -3 \Rightarrow 12x + 9 =$

18) $x = -1 \Rightarrow 9x - 8 =$

19) $x = 2 \Rightarrow 16x - 10 =$

20) $x = 1 \Rightarrow 4x + 3 =$

21) $x = 5 \Rightarrow 7x - 2 =$

22) $x = 7 \Rightarrow 28 - x =$

23) $x = 8 \Rightarrow 4x - 12 =$

24) $x = 10 \Rightarrow 44 - 3x =$

25) $x = 4 \Rightarrow 10x - 6 =$

26) $x = 7 \Rightarrow 6x - x + 9 =$

Evaluating Two Variables

✎ *Evaluate each expression using the values given.*

1) $x + 4y, x = 3, y = 2$ _____

2) $6x + 3y, x = -2, y = -3$ _____

3) $x + 5y, x = 2, y = -1$ _____

4) $3a - (10 - b), a = 3, b = 4$ _____

5) $4a - (6 - 3b), a = 1, b = 4$ _____

6) $a - (8 - 2b), a = 2, b = 5$ _____

7) $3z + 21 + 5k, z = 4, k = 1$ _____

8) $-7a + 4b, a = 6, b = 3$ _____

9) $-4a + 3b, a = 2, b = 4$ _____

10) $-6a + 6b, a = 4, b = 3$ _____

11) $-8a + 2b, a = 4, b = 6$ _____

12) $4x + 6y, x = 6, y = 3$ _____

13) $2x + 9y, x = 8, y = 1$ _____

14) $x - 7y, x = 9, y = 4$ _____

15) $5x - 4y, x = 6, y = 3$ _____

16) $2z + 14 + 8k, z = 4, k = 1$ _____

17) $6x + 3y, x = 3, y = 8$ _____

18) $5a - 6b, a = -3, b = -1$ _____

19) $6a + 2b, a = -6, b = 4$ _____

20) $-3a - b, a = 5, b = -6$ _____

21) $-6a + 2b, a = 6, b = -3$ _____

22) $-6a + 8b, a = 6, b = -1$ _____

The Distributive Property

✍ *Use the distributive property to simply each expression.*

1) $(-2)(10x + 3) =$

2) $(-3x + 5)(-5) =$

3) $11(-3x + 3) =$

4) $6(5 - 4x) =$

5) $(6 - 5x)(-4) =$

6) $9(8 - 2x) =$

7) $(-4x + 6)5 =$

8) $(-2x + 7)(-8) =$

9) $8(-4x + 7) =$

10) $(-9x + 5)(-3) =$

11) $8(-x + 9) =$

12) $7(2 - 6x) =$

13) $(-12x + 4)(-3) =$

14) $(-6)(-10x + 6) =$

15) $(-5)(5 - 11x) =$

16) $9(4 - 8x) =$

17) $(-6x + 2)7 =$

18) $(-9)(1 - 12x) =$

19) $(-3)(4 - 6x) =$

20) $(2 - 8x)(-2) =$

21) $20(2 - x) =$

22) $12(-4x + 3) =$

23) $12(3 - 4x) =$

24) $(-6x + 6)3 =$

25) $(-10x + 6)(-3) =$

26) $13(4 - 7x) =$

Answers – Chapter 6

Simplifying Variable Expressions

1) $9x + 2$

2) $x + 4$

3) $-10x^2 - 1$

4) $-30x + 10$

5) $10x^2 + 2x + 3$

6) $15x^2 + 6x$

7) $2x^2 - 12x$

8) $-2x + 2$

9) $-5x + 14$

10) $-7x^2 + 8x$

11) $5x^2 + 6x$

12) $2x^2 - 3x$

13) $2x^2 + 8x - 6$

14) $-26x + 12$

15) $90x - 48$

16) $-18x - 59$

17) $34x + 19$

18) $-x^2 - 4x + 13$

19) $-38x + 24$

20) $54x - 25$

21) $59x + 24$

22) $-x + 15$

23) $-3x^2 - 15x$

24) $-15x^2 + 22x$

25) $-40x^2 + 74x$

26) $2x^2 + 40x + 12$

27) $5x^2 - 15x - 10$

28) $2x^2 + 16x - 7$

29) $-8x^2 + 6x - 5$

30) $-3x^2 - 10x + 3$

31) $6x^2 + 15x + 18$

32) $6x^2 + 7x + 20$

Simplifying Polynomial Expressions

1) $3x^3 + x^2 - 10x$

2) $-4x^5 - 2x^3 - 5x^2$

3) $18x^4 + 5x^2$

4) $-15x^3 - 8x^2 + 6x$

5) $-7x^3 + 6x^2 - 3$

6) $2x^4 + 13x^3 - 8x$

7) $-15x^3 - 12x^2 + 8x$

8) $-2x^3 - 3x^2 - 2x$

9) $-4x^4 + 2x^3 + x^2 - 2x$

10) $x^4 - 9x^2 - 14x$

11) $3x^4 - 3x^2$

12) $15x^4 - 17x^3 + 4x^2$

13) $10x^4 - 10x^3 + 3x^2$

14) $6x^3 - 4x^2 + 14x$

15) $-6x^5 + 10x^4 - 9x^2$

16) $2x^3 - 4x^2 + 15x$

Evaluating One Variable

1) 0

2) 6

3) 32

4) 16

5) 8

6) 16

7) -3

8) 16

9) -1

10) 13

11) 6

12) -4

13) -68

14) -40

15) 9

16) 29

17) -27

18) -17

19) 22

20) 7

21) 33

22) 21

23) 20

24) 14

25) 34

26) 44

Evaluating Two Variables

1) 11

2) -21

3) -3

4) 3

5) 10

6) 4

7) 38

8) -30

9) 4

10) -6

11) -20

12) 42

13) 25

14) -19

15) 18

16) 30

17) 42

18) -9

19) -28

20) -9

21) -42

22) -44

The Distributive Property

1) $-20x - 6$

2) $15x - 25$

3) $-33x + 33$

4) $-24x + 30$

5) $20x - 24$

6) $-18x + 72$

7) $-20x + 30$

8) $16x - 56$

9) $-32x + 56$

10) $27x - 15$

11) $-8x + 72$

12) $-42x + 14$

13) $36x - 12$

14) $60x - 36$

15) $55x - 25$

16) $-72x + 36$

17) $-42x + 14$

18) $108x - 9$

19) $18x - 12$

20) $16x - 4$

21) $-20x + 40$

22) $-48x + 36$

23) $-48x + 36$

24) $-18x + 18$

25) $30x - 18$

26) $-91x + 52$

Chapter 7: Equations and Inequalities

Math Topics that you'll learn in this Chapter:

- ✓ One–Step Equations
- ✓ Multi–Step Equations
- ✓ System of Equations
- ✓ Graphing Single–Variable Inequalities
- ✓ One–Step Inequalities
- ✓ Multi–Step Inequalities

One–Step Equations

🖎 *Solve each equation for x.*

1) $x - 18 = 28 \Rightarrow x =$ _____

2) $19 = -5 + x \Rightarrow x =$ _____

3) $15 - x = 6 \Rightarrow x =$ _____

4) $x - 24 = 29 \Rightarrow x =$ _____

5) $24 - x = 17 \Rightarrow x =$ _____

6) $16 - x = 3 \Rightarrow x =$ _____

7) $x + 14 = 12 \Rightarrow x =$ _____

8) $26 + x = 8 \Rightarrow x =$ _____

9) $x + 9 = -18 \Rightarrow x =$ _____

10) $x + 21 = 11 \Rightarrow x =$ _____

11) $17 = -5 + x \Rightarrow x =$ _____

12) $x + 20 = 29 \Rightarrow x =$ _____

13) $x - 13 = 19 \Rightarrow x =$ _____

14) $x + 9 = -17 \Rightarrow x =$ _____

15) $x + 4 = -23 \Rightarrow x =$ _____

16) $16 = -9 + x \Rightarrow x =$ _____

17) $4x = 28 \Rightarrow x =$ _____

18) $21 = -7x \Rightarrow x =$ _____

19) $12x = -12 \Rightarrow x =$ _____

20) $13x = 39 \Rightarrow x =$ _____

21) $8x = -16 \Rightarrow x =$ _____

22) $\frac{x}{2} = -5 \Rightarrow x =$ _____

23) $\frac{x}{9} = 6 \Rightarrow x =$ _____

24) $27 = \frac{x}{5} \Rightarrow x =$ _____

25) $\frac{x}{4} = -3 \Rightarrow x =$ _____

26) $x \div 8 = 7 \Rightarrow x =$ _____

27) $x \div 2 = -3 \Rightarrow x =$ _____

28) $8x = 56 \Rightarrow x =$ _____

29) $9x = 54 \Rightarrow x =$ _____

30) $7x = -35 \Rightarrow x =$ _____

31) $60 = -10x \Rightarrow x =$ _____

Multi –Step Equations

✒ *Solve each equation.*

1) $4x - 7 = 13 \Rightarrow x = $ ____

2) $26 = -(x - 4) \Rightarrow x = $ ____

3) $-(5 - x) = 19 \Rightarrow x = $ ____

4) $35 = -x + 14 \Rightarrow x = $ ____

5) $2(3 - 2x) = 10 \Rightarrow x = $ ____

6) $3x - 3 = 15 \Rightarrow x = $ ____

7) $32 = -x + 15 \Rightarrow x = $ ____

8) $-(10 - x) = -13 \Rightarrow x = $ ____

9) $-4(7 + x) = 4 \Rightarrow x = $ ____

10) $22 = 2x - 8 \Rightarrow x = $ ____

11) $-6(3 + x) = 6 \Rightarrow x = $ ____

12) $-3 = 3x - 15 \Rightarrow x = $ ____

13) $-7(12 + x) = 7 \Rightarrow x = $ ____

14) $8(6 - 4x) = 16 \Rightarrow x = $ ____

15) $18 - 4x = -9 - x \Rightarrow x = $ ____

16) $6(4 - x) = 30 \Rightarrow x = $ ____

17) $15 - 3x = -5 - x \Rightarrow x = $ ____

18) $9(-7 - 3x) = 18 \Rightarrow x = $ ____

19) $16 - 2x = -4 - 7x \Rightarrow x = $ ____

20) $14 - 2x = 14 + x \Rightarrow x = $ ____

21) $21 - 3x = -7 - 10x \Rightarrow x = $ __

22) $8 - 2x = 11 + x \Rightarrow x = $ ____

23) $10 + 12x = -8 + 6x \Rightarrow x = $ __

24) $25 + 20x = -5 + 5x \Rightarrow x = $ __

25) $16 - x = -8 - 7x \Rightarrow x = $ ____

26) $17 - 3x = 13 + x \Rightarrow x = $ ____

27) $22 + 5x = -8 - x \Rightarrow x = $ ____

28) $-9(7 + x) = 9 \Rightarrow x = $ ____

29) $12 + 2x = -4 - 2x \Rightarrow x = $ ____

30) $12 - x = 2 - 3x \Rightarrow x = $ ____

31) $19 - x = -1 - 11x \Rightarrow x = $ ____

32) $14 - 3x = -5 - 4x \Rightarrow x = $ ____

Chapter 7: Equations and Inequalities

System of Equations

✍ *Solve each system of equations.*

1) $2x + 3y = 15$ $x =$
   $x - 3y = 3$ $y =$

2) $y = x + 3$ $x =$
   $x + y = -5$ $y =$

3) $x + 3y = 6$ $x =$
   $2x + 8y = -12$ $y =$

4) $2x + y = 5$ $x =$
   $-3x + 6y = 0$ $y =$

5) $10x - 8y = -15$ $x =$
   $-6x + 4y = 13$ $y =$

6) $-3x - 4y = 5$ $x =$
   $x - 2y = 5$ $y =$

7) $5x - 12y = -19$ $x =$
   $-6x + 7y = 8$ $y =$

8) $5x - 7y = -2$ $x =$
   $-x - 2y = -3$ $y =$

9) $-x + 3y = 3$ $x =$
   $-7x + 8y = -5$ $y =$

10) $-4x + 3y = -18$ $x =$
   $4x - y = 14$ $y =$

11) $6x - 7y = -8$ $x =$
   $-x - 4y = -9$ $y =$

12) $-3x + 2y = -16$ $x =$
   $4x - y = 13$ $y =$

13) $2x + 3y = 8$ $x =$
   $-3x + 2y = 1$ $y =$

14) $y = -x + 3$ $x =$
   $3y + 5x = -1$ $y =$

15) $2x + 3y = 12$ $x =$
   $x + y = 5$ $y =$

16) $y = x - 1$ $x =$
   $y = 2x + 2$ $y =$

Graphing Single–Variable Inequalities

✍ *Graph each inequality.*

1) $x < 5$

2) $x \geq 2$

3) $x \geq -4$

4) $x \leq -1$

5) $x > -1$

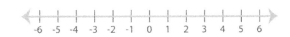

6) $3 > x$

7) $2 \leq x$

8) $x > 0$

9) $-3 \leq x$

10) $-4 \leq x$

11) $x \leq 6$

12) $1 \leq x$

13) $-4 < x$

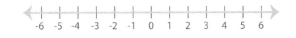

14) $x > -5$

One–Step Inequalities

✎ *Solve each inequality for x.*

1) $x - 9 < 20 \Rightarrow$ _____

2) $14 \leq -6 + x \Rightarrow$ _____

3) $x - 31 > 9 \Rightarrow$ _____

4) $x + 28 \geq 36 \Rightarrow$ _____

5) $x - 24 > 17 \Rightarrow$ _____

6) $x + 5 \geq 3 \Rightarrow x$_____

7) $x + 14 < 12 \Rightarrow$ _____

8) $26 + x \leq 8 \Rightarrow$ _____

9) $x + 9 \geq -18 \Rightarrow$ _____

10) $x + 24 < 11 \Rightarrow$ _____

11) $17 \leq -5 + x \Rightarrow$ _____

12) $x + 25 > 29 \Rightarrow x$_____

13) $x - 17 \geq 19 \Rightarrow$ _____

14) $x + 8 > -17 \Rightarrow$ _____

15) $x + 8 < -23 \Rightarrow$ _____

16) $16 \leq -5 + x \Rightarrow$ _____

17) $4x \leq 12 \Rightarrow$ _____

18) $28 \geq -7x \Rightarrow$ _____

19) $2x > -14 \Rightarrow$ _____

20) $13x \leq 39 \Rightarrow$ _____

21) $-8x > -16 \Rightarrow$ _____

22) $\frac{x}{2} < -6 \Rightarrow$ _____

23) $\frac{x}{6} > 6 \Rightarrow$ _____

24) $27 \leq \frac{x}{4} \Rightarrow$ _____

25) $\frac{x}{8} < -3 \Rightarrow$ _____

26) $6x \geq 18 \Rightarrow$ _____

27) $5x \geq -25 \Rightarrow$ _____

28) $3x > 45 \Rightarrow$ _____

29) $9x \leq 72 \Rightarrow$ _____

30) $-6x < -36 \Rightarrow$ _____

31) $70 > -10x \Rightarrow$ _____

Multi –Step Inequalities

✎ *Solve each inequality.*

1) $2x - 6 \leq 4 \rightarrow$ _____

2) $2 + 3x \geq 17 \rightarrow$ _____

3) $9 + 3x \geq 36 \rightarrow$ _____

4) $2x - 6 \leq 18 \rightarrow$ _____

5) $3x - 4 \leq 23 \rightarrow$ _____

6) $7x - 5 \leq 51 \rightarrow$ _____

7) $4x - 9 \leq 27 \rightarrow$ _____

8) $6x - 11 \leq 13 \rightarrow$ _____

9) $5x - 7 \leq 33 \rightarrow$ _____

10) $6 + 2x \geq 28 \rightarrow$ _____

11) $8 + 3x \geq 35 \rightarrow$ _____

12) $4 + 6x < 34 \rightarrow$ _____

13) $3 + 2x \geq 53 \rightarrow$ _____

14) $7 - 6x > 56 + x \rightarrow$ _____

15) $9 + 4x \geq 39 + 2x \rightarrow$ _____

16) $3 + 5x \geq 43 \rightarrow$ _____

17) $4 - 7x < 60 \rightarrow$ _____

18) $11 - 4x \geq 55 \rightarrow$ _____

19) $12 + x \geq 48 - 2x \rightarrow$ _____

20) $10 - 10x \leq -20 \rightarrow$ _____

21) $5 - 9x \geq -40 \rightarrow$ _____

22) $8 - 7x \geq 36 \rightarrow$ _____

23) $6 + 10x < 69 + 3x \rightarrow$ _____

24) $5 + 4x < 26 - 3x \rightarrow$ _____

25) $10 + 11x < 59 + 4x \rightarrow$ _____

26) $3 + 9x \geq 48 - 6x \rightarrow$ _____

Answers – Chapter 7

One–Step Equations

1) $x = 46$

2) $x = 24$

3) $x = 9$

4) $x = 53$

5) $x = 7$

6) $x = 13$

7) $x = -2$

8) $x = -18$

9) $x = -27$

10) $x = -10$

11) $x = 22$

12) $x = 9$

13) $x = 32$

14) $x = -26$

15) $x = -27$

16) $x = 25$

17) $x = 7$

18) $x = -3$

19) $x = -1$

20) $x = 3$

21) $x = -2$

22) $x = -10$

23) $x = 54$

24) $x = 135$

25) $x = -12$

26) $x = 56$

27) $x = -6$

28) $x = 7$

29) $x = 6$

30) $x = -5$

31) $x = -6$

Multi –Step Equations

1) $x = 5$

2) $x = -22$

3) $x = 24$

4) $x = -21$

5) $x = -1$

6) $x = 6$

7) $x = -17$

8) $x = -3$

9) $x = -8$

10) $x = 15$

11) $x = -4$

12) $x = 4$

13) $x = -13$

14) $x = 1$

15) $x = 9$

16) $x = -1$

17) $x = 10$

18) $x = -3$

19) $x = -4$

20) $x = 0$

21) $x = -4$

22) $x = -1$

23) $x = -3$

24) $x = -2$

25) $x = -4$

26) $x = 1$

27) $x = -5$

28) $x = -8$

29) $x = -4$

30) $x = -5$

31) $x = -2$

32) $x = -19$

System of Equations

1) $x = 6, y = 1$

2) $x = -4, y = -1$

3) $x = 42, y = -12$

4) $x = 2, y = 1$

5) $x = -\frac{11}{2}, y = -5$

6) $x = 1, y = -2$

7) $x = 1, y = 2$

8) $x = 1, y = 1$

9) $x = 3, y = 2$

10) $x = 3, y = -2$

11) $x = 1, y = 2$

12) $x = 2, y = -5$

13) $x = 1, y = 2$

14) $x = -5, y = 8$

15) $x = 3, y = 2$

16) $x = -3, y = -4$

Graphing Single–Variable Inequalities

1) $x < 5$

2) $x \geq 2$

3) $x \geq -4$

4) $x \leq -1$

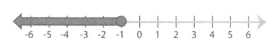

5) $x > -1$

6) $3 > x$

7) $2 \leq x$

8) $x > 0$

9) $-3 \leq x$

10) $-4 \leq x$

11) $x \leq 6$

12) $1 \leq x$

13) $-4 < x$

14) $x > -5$

One–Step Inequalities

1) $x < 29$
2) $20 \le x$
3) $x > 40$
4) $x \ge 8$
5) $x > 41$
6) $x \ge -2$
7) $x < -2$
8) $x \le -18$

9) $x \ge -27$
10) $x < -13$
11) $22 \le x$
12) $x > 4$
13) $x \ge 36$
14) $x > -25$
15) $x < -31$
16) $21 \le x$

17) $x \le 3$
18) $-4 \le x$
19) $x > -7$
20) $x \le 3$
21) $x < 2$
22) $x < -12$
23) $x > 36$
24) $108 \le x$

25) $x < -24$
26) $x \ge 3$
27) $x \ge -5$
28) $x > 15$
29) $x \le 8$
30) $x > 6$
31) $-7 < x$

Multi –Step Inequalities

1) $x \le 5$
2) $x \ge 5$
3) $x \ge 9$
4) $x \le 12$
5) $x \le 9$
6) $x \le 8$
7) $x \le 9$

8) $x \le 4$
9) $x \le 8$
10) $x \ge 11$
11) $x \ge 9$
12) $x < 5$
13) $x \ge 25$
14) $x < -7$

15) $x \ge 15$
16) $x \ge 8$
17) $x > -8$
18) $x \le -11$
19) $x \ge 12$
20) $x \ge 3$
21) $x \le 5$

22) $x \le -4$
23) $x < 9$
24) $x < 3$
25) $x < 7$
26) $x \ge 3$

Chapter 8: Lines and Slope

Math Topics that you'll learn in this Chapter:

- ✓ Finding Slope
- ✓ Graphing Lines Using Slope–Intercept Form
- ✓ Writing Linear Equations
- ✓ Graphing Linear Inequalities
- ✓ Finding Midpoint
- ✓ Finding Distance of Two Points

67

Finding Slope

✎ **Find the slope of each line.**

1) $y = 2x - 8$, Slope =

2) $y = -6x + 3$, Slope =

3) $y = -x - 5$, Slope =

4) $y = -2x - 9$, Slope =

5) $y = 5 + 2x$, Slope =

6) $y = 1 - 8x$, Slope =

7) $y = -4x + 3$, Slope =

8) $y = -9x + 8$, Slope =

9) $y = -2x + 4$, Slope =

10) $y = 9x - 8$, Slope =

11) $y = \frac{1}{2}x + 4$, Slope =

12) $y = -\frac{2}{5}x + 7$, Slope =

13) $-x + 3y = 5$, Slope =

14) $4x + 4y = 6$, Slope =

15) $6y - 2x = 10$, Slope =

16) $3y - x = 2$, Slope =

✎ **Find the slope of the line through each pair of points.**

17) $(4, 4), (8, 12)$, Slope =

23) $(8, 4), (9, 6)$, Slope =

18) $(-2, 4), (0, 6)$, Slope =

24) $(10, -1), (7, 8)$, Slope =

19) $(6, -2), (2, 6)$, Slope =

25) $(16, -3), (13, -6)$, Slope =

20) $(-4, -2), (0, 6)$, Slope =

26) $(12, 5), (8, 1)$, Slope =

21) $(6, 2), (3, 5)$, Slope =

27) $(6, 6), (8, 10)$, Slope =

22) $(-5, 1), (-1, 9)$, Slope =

28) $(10, -1), (8, 1)$, Slope =

Graphing Lines Using Slope–Intercept Form

✎ *Sketch the graph of each line.*

1) $y = -x + 1$

2) $y = 2x - 4$

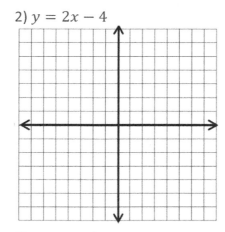

3) $y = -x + 6$

4) $y = x - 4$

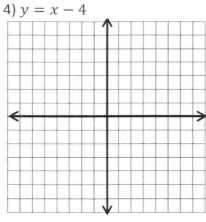

5) $y = 2x - 2$

6) $y = -\frac{1}{2}x + 2$

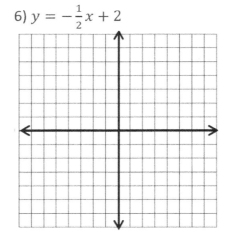

Writing Linear Equations

✎ *Write the equation of the line through the given points.*

1) through: $(2, -2), (3, 4)$ $y =$

2) through: $(-2, 4), (1, 7)$ $y =$

3) through: $(-1, 3), (3, 7)$ $y =$

4) through: $(6, 5), (3, 2)$ $y =$

5) through: $(7, -10), (2, 10)$ $y =$

6) through: $(7, 2), (6, 1)$ $y =$

7) through: $(6, -1), (4, 1)$ $y =$

8) through: $(-2, 8), (-4, -6)$ $y =$

9) through: $(-2, 5), (-3, 4)$ $y =$

10) through: $(6, 8), (8, -6)$ $y =$

11) through: $(-2, 5), (-4, -3)$ $y =$

12) through: $(8, 8), (4, -8)$ $y =$

13) through: $(7, -4)$, Slope: -1 $y =$

14) through: $(4, -10)$, Slope: -2 $y =$

15) through: $(6, 10)$, Slope: 9 $y =$

16) through: $(-6, 8)$, Slope: -2 $y =$

✎ *Solve each problem.*

17) What is the equation of a line with slope 6 and intercept 4? _____

18) What is the equation of a line with slope 5 and intercept 9? _____

19) What is the equation of a line with slope 8 and passes through point $(2, 8)$?

_____

20) What is the equation of a line with slope -3 and passes through point

$(-4, 10)$? _____

Chapter 8: Lines and Slope

Finding Midpoint

✎ *Find the midpoint of the line segment with the given endpoints.*

1) $(4, 4), (0, 4),$ $midpoint = (\_\_, \_\_)$

2) $(5, 1), (-1, 5),$ $midpoint = (\_\_, \_\_)$

3) $(4, -2), (0, 6),$ $midpoint = (\_\_, \_\_)$

4) $(-3, 3), (-1, 5),$ $midpoint = (\_\_, \_\_)$

5) $(5, -2), (9, -6),$ $midpoint = (\_\_, \_\_)$

6) $(-6, -3), (4, -7),$ $midpoint = (\_\_, \_\_)$

7) $(7, 0), (-7, 8),$ $midpoint = (\_\_, \_\_)$

8) $(-8, 4), (-4, 0),$ $midpoint = (\_\_, \_\_)$

9) $(-3, 6), (9, -8),$ $midpoint = (\_\_, \_\_)$

10) $(6, 8), (6, -6),$ $midpoint = (\_\_, \_\_)$

11) $(6, 7), (-8, 5),$ $midpoint = (\_\_, \_\_)$

12) $(9, 3), (-3, -9),$ $midpoint = (\_\_, \_\_)$

13) $(-6, 12), (-4, 6),$ $midpoint = (\_\_, \_\_)$

14) $(10, 7), (8, -3),$ $midpoint = (\_\_, \_\_)$

15) $(13, 7), (-5, 3),$ $midpoint = (\_\_, \_\_)$

16) $(-9, -4), (-5, 8),$ $midpoint = (\_\_, \_\_)$

17) $(12, 5), (6, 15),$ $midpoint = (\_\_, \_\_)$

18) $(-6, -10), (12, -2),$ $midpoint = (\_\_, \_\_)$

19) $(14, 13), (-4, 9),$ $midpoint = (\_\_, \_\_)$

20) $(10, -4), (8, 12),$ $midpoint = (\_\_, \_\_)$

Finding Distance of Two Points

✎ *Find the distance of each pair of points.*

1) $(0, 9), (4, 6),$

   Distance = ____

2) $(-4, 6), (8, 11),$

   Distance = ____

3) $(-6, 1), (-3, 5),$

   Distance = ____

4) $(-3, 2), (3, 10),$

   Distance = ____

5) $(-5, 3), (4, -9),$

   Distance = ____

6) $(-7, -5), (5, 0),$

   Distance = ____

7) $(4, 3), (-4, -12),$

   Distance = ____

8) $(10, 1), (-5, -19),$

   Distance = ____

9) $(3, 3), (-1, 5),$

   Distance = ____

10) $(2, -1), (10, 5),$

   Distance = ____

11) $(-3, 7), (-1, 4),$

   Distance = ____

12) $(5, -2), (9, -5),$

   Distance = ____

13) $(-8, 4), (4, 9),$

   Distance = ____

14) $(6, 8), (6, -6),$

   Distance = ____

15) $(6, -6), (0, 2),$

   Distance = ____

16) $(-4, 10), (-4, 4),$

   Distance = ____

17) $(-7, -6), (-2, 6),$

   Distance = ____

18) $(11, 0), (3, 15),$

   Distance = ____

Answers – Chapter 8

Finding Slope

1) 2	7) -4	13) $\frac{1}{3}$	18) 1	24) -3
2) -6	8) -9	14) -1	19) -2	25) 1
3) -1	9) -2	15) $\frac{1}{3}$	20) 2	26) 1
4) -2	10) 9	16) $\frac{1}{3}$	21) -1	27) 2
5) 2	11) $\frac{1}{2}$	17) 2	22) 2	28) -1
6) -8	12) $-\frac{2}{5}$		23) 2	

Graphing Lines Using Slope–Intercept Form

1) $y = -x + 1$

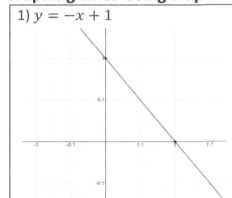

2) $y = 2x - 4$

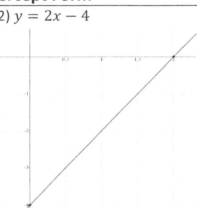

3) $y = -x + 6$

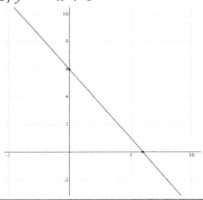

4) $y = x - 4$

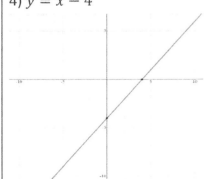

5) $y = 2x - 2$

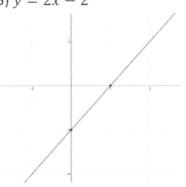

6) $y = -\frac{1}{2}x + 2$

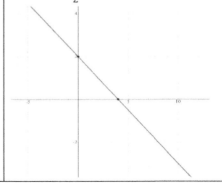

Writing Linear Equations

1) $y = 6x - 14$

2) $y = x + 6$

3) $y = x + 4$

4) $y = x - 1$

5) $y = -4x + 18$

6) $y = x - 5$

7) $y = -x + 5$

8) $y = 7x + 22$

9) $y = x + 7$

10) $y = -7x + 50$

11) $y = 4x + 13$

12) $y = 4x - 24$

13) $y = -x + 3$

14) $y = -2x - 2$

15) $y = 9x - 44$

16) $y = -2x - 4$

17) $y = 6x + 4$

18) $y = 5x + 9$

19) $y = 8x - 8$

20) $y = -3x - 2$

Finding Midpoint

1) $midpoint = (2, 4)$

2) $midpoint = (2, 3)$

3) $midpoint = (2, 2)$

4) $midpoint = (-2, 4)$

5) $midpoint = (7, -4)$

6) $midpoint = (-1, -5)$

7) $midpoint = (0, 4)$

8) $midpoint = (-6, 2)$

9) $midpoint = (3, -1)$

10) $midpoint = (6, 1)$

11) $midpoint = (-1, 6)$

12) $midpoint = (3, -3)$

13) $midpoint = (-5, 9)$

14) $midpoint = (9, 2)$

15) $midpoint = (4, 5)$

16) $midpoint = (-7, 2)$

17) $midpoint = (9, 10)$

18) $midpoint = (3, -6)$

19) $midpoint = (5, 11)$

20) $midpoint = (9, 4)$

Finding Distance of Two Points

1) Distance $= 5$

2) Distance $= 13$

3) Distance $= 5$

4) Distance $= 10$

5) Distance $= 15$

6) Distance $= 13$

7) Distance $= 17$

8) Distance $= 25$

9) Distance $= \sqrt{20} = 2\sqrt{5}$

10) Distance $= 10$

11) Distance $= \sqrt{13}$

12) Distance $= 5$

13) Distance $= 13$

14) Distance $= 14$

15) Distance $= 10$

16) Distance $= 6$

17) Distance $= 13$

18) Distance $= 17$

Chapter 9: Exponents and Variables

Math Topics that you'll learn in this Chapter:

- ✓ Multiplication Property of Exponents
- ✓ Division Property of Exponents
- ✓ Powers of Products and Quotients
- ✓ Zero and Negative Exponents
- ✓ Negative Exponents and Negative Bases
- ✓ Scientific Notation
- ✓ Radicals

77

Multiplication Property of Exponents

✎ *Simplify and write the answer in exponential form.*

1) $3 \times 3^2 =$

2) $4^3 \times 4 =$

3) $2^2 \times 2^2 =$

4) $6^2 \times 6^2 =$

5) $7^3 \times 7^2 \times 7 =$

6) $2 \times 2^2 \times 2^2 =$

7) $5^3 \times 5^2 \times 5 \times 5 =$

8) $2x \times x =$

9) $x^3 \times x^2 =$

10) $x^4 \times x^4 =$

11) $x^2 \times x^2 \times x^2 =$

12) $6x \times 6x =$

13) $2x^2 \times 2x^2 =$

14) $3x^2 \times x =$

15) $4x^4 \times 4x^4 \times 4x^4 =$

16) $2x^2 \times x^2 =$

17) $x^4 \times 3x =$

18) $x \times 2x^2 =$

19) $5x^4 \times 5x^4 =$

20) $2yx^2 \times 2x =$

21) $3x^4 \times y^2x^4 =$

22) $y^2x^3 \times y^5x^2 =$

23) $4yx^3 \times 2x^2y^3 =$

24) $6x^2 \times 6x^3y^4 =$

25) $3x^4y^5 \times 7x^2y^3 =$

26) $7x^2y^5 \times 9xy^3 =$

27) $7xy^4 \times 4x^3y^3 =$

28) $3x^5y^3 \times 8x^2y^3 =$

29) $6x \times y^5x^2 \times y^3 =$

30) $yx^3 \times 3y^3x^2 \times 2xy =$

31) $5yx^3 \times 4y^2x \times xy^3 =$

32) $6x^2 \times 3x^3y^4 \times 10yx^3 =$

Division Property of Exponents

✎ *Simplify and write the answer.*

1) $\dfrac{3^2}{3^3} =$

2) $\dfrac{2^6}{2^2} =$

3) $\dfrac{4^4}{4} =$

4) $\dfrac{5}{5^4} =$

5) $\dfrac{x}{x^3} =$

6) $\dfrac{3 \times 3^3}{3^2 \times 3^4} =$

7) $\dfrac{5^8}{5^3} =$

8) $\dfrac{5 \times 5^6}{5^2 \times 5^7} =$

9) $\dfrac{3^4 \times 3^7}{3^2 \times 3^8} =$

10) $\dfrac{5x}{10x^3} =$

11) $\dfrac{5x^3}{2x^5} =$

12) $\dfrac{18x^3}{14x^6} =$

13) $\dfrac{12x^3}{8xy^8} =$

14) $\dfrac{24xy^3}{4x^4y^2} =$

15) $\dfrac{21x^3y^9}{7xy^5} =$

16) $\dfrac{36x^2y^9}{4x^3} =$

17) $\dfrac{18x^3y^4}{10x^6y^8} =$

18) $\dfrac{16y^2x^{14}}{24yx^8} =$

19) $\dfrac{15x^4y}{9x^9y^2} =$

20) $\dfrac{7x^7y^2}{28x^5y^6} =$

Chapter 9: Exponents and Variables

Powers of Products and Quotients

✎ *Simplify and write the answer.*

1) $(3^2)^2 =$

2) $(5^2)^3 =$

3) $(3 \times 3^3)^4 =$

4) $(6 \times 6^4)^2 =$

5) $(3^3 \times 3^2)^3 =$

6) $(5^4 \times 5^5)^2 =$

7) $(2 \times 2^4)^2 =$

8) $(2x^6)^2 =$

9) $(11x^5)^2 =$

10) $(4x^2y^4)^4 =$

11) $(2x^4y^4)^3 =$

12) $(3x^2y^2)^2 =$

13) $(3x^4y^3)^4 =$

14) $(2x^6y^8)^2 =$

15) $(12x^3x)^3 =$

16) $(5x^9x^6)^3 =$

17) $(5x^{10}y^3)^3 =$

18) $(14x^3x^3)^2 =$

19) $(3x^3 5x)^2 =$

20) $(10x^{11}y^3)^2 =$

21) $(9x^7y^5)^2 =$

22) $(4x^4y^6)^5 =$

23) $(3x4y^3)^2 =$

24) $\left(\frac{6x}{x^2}\right)^2 =$

25) $\left(\frac{x^5y^5}{x^2y^2}\right)^3 =$

26) $\left(\frac{24x}{4x^6}\right)^2 =$

27) $\left(\frac{x^5}{x^6y^2}\right)^2 =$

28) $\left(\frac{xy^3}{x^2y^5}\right)^3 =$

29) $\left(\frac{3xy^3}{x^4}\right)^2 =$

30) $\left(\frac{xy^5}{4xy^3}\right)^3 =$

Zero and Negative Exponents

✏️ *Evaluate the following expressions.*

1) $2^{-1} =$

2) $3^{-2} =$

3) $0^{10} =$

4) $1^{-8} =$

5) $8^{-1} =$

6) $8^{-2} =$

7) $2^{-4} =$

8) $10^{-2} =$

9) $9^{-2} =$

10) $3^{-3} =$

11) $7^{-3} =$

12) $3^{-4} =$

13) $6^{-3} =$

14) $5^{-3} =$

15) $22^{-1} =$

16) $4^{-4} =$

17) $5^{-4} =$

18) $15^{-2} =$

19) $4^{-5} =$

20) $9^{-3} =$

21) $3^{-5} =$

22) $5^{-4} =$

23) $12^{-2} =$

24) $15^{-3} =$

25) $20^{-3} =$

26) $50^{-2} =$

27) $18^{-3} =$

28) $24^{-2} =$

29) $30^{-3} =$

30) $10^{-5} =$

31) $\left(\frac{1}{8}\right)^{-1} =$

32) $\left(\frac{1}{5}\right)^{-2} =$

33) $\left(\frac{1}{7}\right)^{-2} =$

34) $\left(\frac{2}{3}\right)^{-2} =$

35) $\left(\frac{1}{5}\right)^{-3} =$

36) $\left(\frac{3}{4}\right)^{-2} =$

37) $\left(\frac{2}{5}\right)^{-2} =$

38) $\left(\frac{1}{2}\right)^{-8} =$

39) $\left(\frac{2}{3}\right)^{-3} =$

40) $\left(\frac{3}{4}\right)^{-3} =$

41) $\left(\frac{5}{6}\right)^{-2} =$

42) $\left(\frac{6}{9}\right)^{-2} =$

Negative Exponents and Negative Bases

✎ *Simplify and write the answer.*

1) $-2^{-1} =$

2) $-4^{-2} =$

3) $-3^{-4} =$

4) $-x^{-5} =$

5) $2x^{-1} =$

6) $-4x^{-3} =$

7) $-12x^{-5} =$

8) $-5x^{-2}y^{-3} =$

9) $20x^{-4}y^{-1} =$

10) $14a^{-6}b^{-7} =$

11) $-12x^2y^{-3} =$

12) $-\dfrac{25}{x^{-6}} =$

13) $-\dfrac{2x}{y^{-4}} =$

14) $(-\dfrac{1}{3x})^{-2} =$

15) $(-\dfrac{3}{4x})^{-2} =$

16) $-\dfrac{9}{a^{-7}b^{-2}} =$

17) $-\dfrac{5x}{x^{-3}} =$

18) $-\dfrac{a^{-3}}{b^{-2}} =$

19) $-\dfrac{8}{x^{-3}} =$

20) $\dfrac{5b}{-9c^{-4}} =$

21) $\dfrac{9ab}{a^{-3}b^{-1}} =$

22) $-\dfrac{15a^{-2}}{30b^{-3}} =$

23) $\dfrac{4ab^{-2}}{-3c^{-2}} =$

24) $(\dfrac{3a}{2c})^{-2} =$

25) $(-\dfrac{3x}{4yz})^{-2} =$

26) $\dfrac{15ab^{-6}}{-9c^{-2}} =$

27) $(-\dfrac{x^3}{x^4})^{-3} =$

28) $(-\dfrac{x^{-2}}{2x^2})^{-2} =$

Scientific Notation

✎ **Write each number in scientific notation.**

1) $0.114 =$

2) $0.06 =$

3) $8.6 =$

4) $30 =$

5) $60 =$

6) $0.004 =$

7) $78 =$

8) $1,600 =$

9) $1,450 =$

10) $31,000 =$

11) $2,000,000 =$

12) $0.0000003 =$

13) $554,000 =$

14) $0.000725 =$

15) $0.00034 =$

16) $86,000,000 =$

17) $62,000 =$

18) $97,000,000 =$

19) $0.0000045 =$

20) $0.0019 =$

✎ **Write each number in standard notation.**

21) $2 \times 10^{-1} =$

22) $8 \times 10^{-2} =$

23) $1.8 \times 10^3 =$

24) $9 \times 10^{-4} =$

25) $1.7 \times 10^{-2} =$

26) $9 \times 10^3 =$

27) $6 \times 10^4 =$

28) $2.18 \times 10^5 =$

29) $5 \times 10^{-3} =$

30) $9.4 \times 10^{-5} =$

Radicals

✍ *Simplify and write the answer.*

1) $\sqrt{1} =$ ____

2) $\sqrt{0} =$ ____

3) $\sqrt{16} =$ ____

4) $\sqrt{4} =$ ____

5) $\sqrt{9} =$ ____

6) $\sqrt{25} =$ ____

7) $\sqrt{49} =$ ____

8) $\sqrt{36} =$ ____

9) $\sqrt{64} =$ ____

10) $\sqrt{81} =$ ____

11) $\sqrt{121} =$ ____

12) $\sqrt{225} =$ ____

13) $\sqrt{144} =$ ____

14) $\sqrt{100} =$ ____

15) $\sqrt{256} =$ ____

16) $\sqrt{289} =$ ____

17) $\sqrt{324} =$ ____

18) $\sqrt{400} =$ ____

19) $\sqrt{900} =$ ____

20) $\sqrt{529} =$ ____

21) $\sqrt{361} =$ ____

22) $\sqrt{169} =$ ____

23) $\sqrt{196} =$ ____

24) $\sqrt{90} =$ ____

✍ *Evaluate.*

25) $\sqrt{6} \times \sqrt{6} =$

26) $\sqrt{5} \times \sqrt{5} =$

27) $\sqrt{8} \times \sqrt{8} =$

28) $\sqrt{2} + \sqrt{2} =$

29) $\sqrt{8} + \sqrt{8} =$

30) $6\sqrt{5} - 2\sqrt{5} =$

31) $\sqrt{25} \times \sqrt{16} =$

32) $\sqrt{25} \times \sqrt{64} =$

33) $\sqrt{64} \times \sqrt{49} =$

34) $5\sqrt{5} \times 3\sqrt{5} =$

35) $7\sqrt{3} \times 2\sqrt{3} =$

36) $5\sqrt{2} - \sqrt{8} =$

Answers – Chapter 9

Multiplication Property of Exponents

1) 3^3

2) 4^4

3) 2^4

4) 6^4

5) 7^6

6) 2^5

7) 5^7

8) $2x^2$

9) x^5

10) x^8

11) x^6

12) $36x^2$

13) $4x^4$

14) $3x^3$

15) $64x^{12}$

16) $2x^4$

17) $3x^5$

18) $2x^3$

19) $25x^8$

20) $4x^3y$

21) $3x^8y^2$

22) x^5y^7

23) $8x^5y^4$

24) $36x^5y^4$

25) $21x^6y^8$

26) $63x^3y^8$

27) $28x^4y^7$

28) $24x^7y^6$

29) $6x^3y^8$

30) $6x^6y^5$

31) $20x^5y^6$

32) $180x^8y^5$

Division Property of Exponents

1) $\frac{1}{3}$

2) 2^4

3) 4^3

4) $\frac{1}{5^3}$

5) $\frac{1}{x^2}$

6) $\frac{1}{3^2}$

7) 5^5

8) $\frac{1}{5^2}$

9) 3

10) $\frac{1}{2x^2}$

11) $\frac{5}{2x^2}$

12) $\frac{9}{7x^3}$

13) $\frac{3x^2}{2y^8}$

14) $\frac{6y}{x^3}$

15) $3x^2y^4$

16) $\frac{9y^9}{x}$

17) $\frac{9}{5x^3y^4}$

18) $\frac{2yx^6}{3}$

19) $\frac{5}{3x^5y}$

20) $\frac{x^2}{4y^4}$

Powers of Products and Quotients

1) 3^4

2) 5^6

3) 3^{16}

4) 6^{10}

5) 3^{15}

6) 5^{18}

7) 2^{10}

8) $4x^{12}$

9) $121x^{10}$

10) $256x^8y^{16}$

11) $8x^{12}y^{12}$

12) $9x^4y^4$

13) $81x^{16}y^{12}$

14) $4x^{12}y^{16}$

15) $1{,}728x^{12}$

16) $125x^{45}$

17) $125x^{30}y^9$

18) $196x^{12}$

19) $225x^8$

20) $100x^{22}y^6$

21) $81x^{14}y^{10}$

22) $1{,}024x^{20}y^{30}$

23) $144x^2y^6$

24) $\dfrac{36}{x^2}$

25) x^9y^9

26) $\dfrac{36}{x^{10}}$

27) $\dfrac{1}{x^2y^4}$

28) $\dfrac{1}{x^3y^6}$

29) $\dfrac{9y^6}{x^6}$

30) $\dfrac{y^6}{64}$

Zero and Negative Exponents

1) $\frac{1}{2}$

2) $\frac{1}{9}$

3) 0

4) 1

5) $\frac{1}{8}$

6) $\frac{1}{64}$

7) $\frac{1}{16}$

8) $\frac{1}{100}$

9) $\frac{1}{81}$

10) $\frac{1}{27}$

11) $\frac{1}{343}$

12) $\frac{1}{81}$

13) $\frac{1}{216}$

14) $\frac{1}{125}$

15) $\frac{1}{22}$

16) $\frac{1}{256}$

17) $\frac{1}{625}$

18) $\frac{1}{225}$

19) $\frac{1}{1,024}$

20) $\frac{1}{729}$

21) $\frac{1}{243}$

22) $\frac{1}{625}$

23) $\frac{1}{144}$

24) $\frac{1}{3,375}$

25) $\frac{1}{8,000}$

26) $\frac{1}{2,500}$

27) $\frac{1}{5,832}$

28) $\frac{1}{576}$

29) $\frac{1}{27,000}$

30) $\frac{1}{100,000}$

31) 8

32) 25

33) 49

34) $\frac{9}{4}$

35) 125

36) $\frac{16}{9}$

37) $\frac{25}{4}$

38) 256

39) $\frac{27}{8}$

40) $\frac{64}{27}$

41) $\frac{36}{25}$

42) $\frac{81}{36}$

Negative Exponents and Negative Bases

1) $-\dfrac{1}{2}$

2) $-\dfrac{1}{16}$

3) $-\dfrac{1}{81}$

4) $-\dfrac{1}{x^5}$

5) $\dfrac{2}{x}$

6) $-\dfrac{4}{x^3}$

7) $-\dfrac{12}{x^5}$

8) $-\dfrac{5}{x^2 y^3}$

9) $\dfrac{20}{x^4 y}$

10) $\dfrac{14}{a^6 b^7}$

11) $-\dfrac{12x^2}{y^3}$

12) $-25x^6$

13) $-2xy^4$

14) $9x^2$

15) $\dfrac{16x^2}{9}$

16) $-9a^7 b^2$

17) $-5x^4$

18) $-\dfrac{b^2}{a^3}$

19) $-8x^3$

20) $-\dfrac{5bc^4}{9}$

21) $9a^4 b^2$

22) $-\dfrac{b^3}{2a^2}$

23) $-\dfrac{4ac^2}{3b^2}$

24) $\dfrac{4c^2}{9a^2}$

25) $\dfrac{16y^2 z^2}{9x^2}$

26) $-\dfrac{5ac^2}{3b^6}$

27) $-x^3$

28) $4x^8$

Scientific Notation

1) 1.14×10^{-1}

2) 6×10^{-2}

3) 8.6×10^{0}

4) 3×10^{1}

5) 6×10^{1}

6) 4×10^{-3}

7) 7.8×10^{1}

8) 1.6×10^{3}

9) 1.45×10^{3}

10) 3.1×10^{4}

11) 2×10^{6}

12) 3×10^{-7}

13) 5.54×10^{5}

14) 7.25×10^{-4}

15) 3.4×10^{-4}

16) 8.6×10^{7}

17) 6.2×10^{4}

18) 9.7×10^{7}

19) 4.5×10^{-6}

20) 1.9×10^{-3}

21) 0.2

22) 0.08

23) $1,800$

24) 0.0009

25) 0.017

26) $9,000$

27) $60,000$

28) $218,000$

29) 0.005

30) 0.000094

Radicals

1) 1

2) 0

3) 4

4) 2

5) 3

6) 5

7) 7

8) 6

9) 8

10) 9

11) 11

12) 15

13) 12

14) 10

15) 16

16) 17

17) 18

18) 20

19) 30

20) 23

21) 19

22) 13

23) 14

24) $3\sqrt{10}$

25) 6

26) 5

27) 8

28) $2\sqrt{2}$

29) $2\sqrt{8} = 4\sqrt{2}$

30) $4\sqrt{5}$

31) 20

32) 40

33) 56

34) 75

35) 42

36) $3\sqrt{2}$

Chapter 10:

Polynomials

Math Topics that you'll learn in this Chapter:

- ✓ Simplifying Polynomials
- ✓ Adding and Subtracting Polynomials
- ✓ Multiplying Monomials
- ✓ Multiplying and Dividing Monomials
- ✓ Multiplying a Polynomial and a Monomial
- ✓ Multiplying Binomials
- ✓ Factoring Trinomials

91

Chapter 10: Polynomials

Simplifying Polynomials

✍ *Simplify each expression.*

1) $3(2x + 1) =$ _____

2) $2(4x - 6) =$ _____

3) $4(3x + 3) =$ _____

4) $2(4x + 5) =$ _____

5) $-3(8x - 7) =$ _____

6) $2x(3x + 4) =$ _____

7) $3x^2 + 3x^2 - 2x^3 =$ _____

8) $2x - x^2 + 6x^3 + 4 =$ _____

9) $5x + 2x^2 - 9x^3 =$ _____

10) $7x^2 + 5x^4 - 2x^3 =$ _____

11) $-3x^2 + 5x^3 + 6x^4 =$ _____

12) $(x - 3)(x - 4) =$ _____

13) $(x - 5)(x + 4) =$ _____

14) $(x - 6)(x - 3) =$ _____

15) $(2x + 5)(x + 8) =$ _____

16) $(3x - 8)(x + 4) =$ _____

17) $-8x^2 + 2x^3 - 10x^4 + 5x =$ _____

18) $11 - 6x^2 + 5x^2 - 12x^3 + 22 =$ _____

19) $3x^2 - 4x + 4x^3 + 10x - 21x =$ _____

20) $10 - 6x^2 + 5x^2 - 3x^3 + 2 =$ _____

21) $3x^5 - 2x^3 + 8x^2 - x^5 =$ _____

22) $(5x^3 - 1) + (4x^3 - 6x^3) =$ _____

Adding and Subtracting Polynomials

✍ *Add or subtract expressions.*

1) $(x^2 - 5) + (x^2 + 6) = $ _____

2) $(2x^2 - 6) - (3 - 2x^2) = $ _____

3) $(x^3 + 3x^2) - (x^3 + 6) = $ _____

4) $(4x^3 - x^2) + (6x^2 - 8x) = $ _____

5) $(2x^3 + 3x) - (5x^3 + 2) = $ _____

6) $(5x^3 - 2) + (2x^3 + 10) = $ _____

7) $(7x^3 + 5) - (9 - 4x^3) = $ _____

8) $(5x^2 + 3x^3) - (2x^3 + 6) = $ _____

9) $(8x^2 - x) + (4x - 8x^2) = $ _____

10) $(6x + 9x^2) - (5x + 2) = $ _____

11) $(7x^4 - 2x) - (6x - 2x^4) = $ _____

12) $(2x - 4x^3) - (9x^3 + 6x) = $ _____

13) $(8x^3 - 8x^2) - (6x^2 - 3x) = $ _____

14) $(9x^2 - 6) + (5x^2 - 4x^3) = $ _____

15) $(8x^3 + 3x^4) - (x^4 - 3x^3) = $ _____

16) $(-4x^3 - 2x) + (5x - 2x^3) = $ _____

17) $(9x - 5x^4) - (8x^4 + 4x) = $ _____

18) $(8x - 3x^2) - (7x^4 - 3x^2) = $ _____

19) $(9x^3 - 7) + (5x^3 - 4x^2) = $ _____

20) $(7x^3 + x^4) - (6x^4 - 5x^3) = $ _____

Multiplying Monomials

✎ *Simplify each expression.*

1) $4x^7 \times x^3 =$

_____

2) $6y^2 \times 6y^3 =$

_____

3) $-6z^7 \times 4z^4 =$

_____

4) $5x^5y \times 8xy^3 =$

_____

5) $-6xy^8 \times 3x^5y^3 =$

_____

6) $7a^4b^2 \times 3a^8b =$

_____

7) $5xy^5 \times 3x^3y^4 =$

_____

8) $5p^5q^4 \times (-6pq^4) =$

_____

9) $8s^6t^2 \times 6s^3t^7 =$

_____

10) $(-8x^5y^2) \times 4x^6y^3 =$

_____

11) $9xy^6z \times 3y^4z^2 =$

_____

12) $12x^5y^4 \times 2x^8y =$

_____

13) $4pq^5 \times (-7p^4q^8) =$

_____

14) $9s^4t^2 \times (-5st^5) =$

_____

15) $10p^3q^5 \times (-4p^4q^6) =$

_____

16) $(-5p^2q^4r) \times 7pq^5r^3 =$

_____

17) $(-9a^4b^7c^4) \times (-4a^7b) =$

_____

18) $7u^5v^9 \times (-5u^{12}v^7) =$

_____

19) $4u^4v^9z^2 \times (-5uv^8z) =$

_____

20) $(-6xy^3z^5) \times 3x^3yz^7 =$

_____

21) $6x^2y^3z^5 \times (-7x^4y^2z) =$

_____

22) $7a^5b^8c^{12} \times 4a^6b^5c^9 =$

_____

Multiplying and Dividing Monomials

✎ *Simplify each expression.*

1) $(3x^5)(2x^2) =$

_____

2) $(6x^5)(2x^4) =$

_____

3) $(-7x^9)(2x^5) =$

_____

4) $(7x^7y^9)(-5x^6y^6) =$

_____

5) $(8x^5y^6)(3x^2y^5) =$

_____

6) $(8yx^2)(7y^5x^3) =$

_____

7) $(4x^2y)(2x^2y^3) =$

_____

8) $(-2x^9y^4)(-9x^6y^8) =$

_____

9) $(-5x^8y^2)(-6x^4y^5) =$

_____

10) $(8x^8y)(-7x^4y^3) =$

_____

11) $(9x^6y^2)(6x^7y^4) =$

_____

12) $(8x^9y^5)(6x^5y^4) =$

_____

13) $(-5x^8y^9)(7x^7y^8) =$

_____

14) $(6x^2y^5)(5x^3y^2) =$

_____

15) $(9x^5y^{12})(4x^7y^9) =$

_____

16) $(-10x^{14}y^8)(2x^7y^5) =$

_____

17) $\frac{6x^5y^7}{xy^6} =$

_____

18) $\frac{9x^6y^6}{3x^4y} =$

_____

19) $\frac{16x^4y^6}{4xy} =$

_____

20) $\frac{-30x^9y^8}{5x^5y^4} =$

_____

Multiplying a Polynomial and a Monomial

✐ *Find each product.*

1) $x(x - 5) =$
_____

2) $2(3 + x) =$
_____

3) $x(x - 7) =$
_____

4) $x(x + 9) =$
_____

5) $2x(x - 2) =$
_____

6) $5(4x + 3) =$
_____

7) $4x(3x - 4) =$
_____

8) $x(5x + 2y) =$
_____

9) $3x(x - 2y) =$
_____

10) $6x(3x - 4y) =$
_____

11) $2x(3x - 8) =$
_____

12) $6x(4x - 6y) =$
_____

13) $3x(4x - 2y) =$
_____

14) $2x(2x - 6y) =$
_____

15) $5x(x^2 + y^2) =$
_____

16) $3x(2x^2 - y^2) =$
_____

17) $6(9x^2 + 3y^2) =$
_____

18) $4x(-3x^2y + 2y) =$
_____

19) $-3(6x^2 - 5xy + 3) =$
_____

20) $6(x^2 - 4xy - 3) =$
_____

Multiplying Binomials

✎ *Find each product.*

1) $(x - 3)(x + 4) =$

_____

2) $(x + 3)(x + 5) =$

_____

3) $(x - 6)(x - 7) =$

_____

4) $(x - 9)(x - 4) =$

_____

5) $(x - 7)(x - 5) =$

_____

6) $(x + 6)(x + 2) =$

_____

7) $(x - 9)(x + 3) =$

_____

8) $(x - 8)(x - 5) =$

_____

9) $(x + 3)(x + 7) =$

_____

10) $(x - 9)(x + 4) =$

_____

11) $(x + 6)(x + 6) =$

_____

12) $(x + 7)(x + 7) =$

_____

13) $(x - 8)(x + 7) =$

_____

14) $(x + 9)(x + 9) =$

_____

15) $(x - 8)(x - 8) =$

_____

16) $(x - 9)(x + 5) =$

_____

17) $(2x - 5)(x + 4) =$

_____

18) $(2x + 6)(x + 3) =$

_____

19) $(2x + 4)(x + 5) =$

_____

20) $(2x - 3)(2x + 2) =$

_____

Factoring Trinomials

✎ *Factor each trinomial.*

1) $x^2 + 5x + 4 =$

_____

2) $x^2 + 5x + 6 =$

_____

3) $x^2 - 4x + 3 =$

4) $x^2 - 10x + 25 =$

_____

5) $x^2 - 13x + 40 =$

_____

6) $x^2 + 8x + 12 =$

7) $x^2 - 6x - 27 =$

_____

8) $x^2 - 14x + 48 =$

_____

9) $x^2 + 15x + 56 =$

_____

10) $x^2 - 5x - 36 =$

_____

11) $x^2 + 12x + 36 =$

_____

12) $x^2 + 16x + 63 =$

_____

13) $x^2 + x - 72 =$

_____

14) $x^2 + 18x + 81 =$

_____

15) $x^2 - 16x + 64 =$

_____

16) $x^2 - 18x + 81 =$

_____

17) $2x^2 + 10x + 8 =$

_____

18) $2x^2 + 4x - 6 =$

_____

19) $2x^2 + 9x + 4 =$

_____

20) $4x^2 + 4x - 24 =$

_____

Answers – Chapter 10

Simplifying Polynomials

1) $6x + 3$

2) $8x - 12$

3) $12x + 12$

4) $8x + 10$

5) $-24x + 21$

6) $6x^2 + 8x$

7) $-2x^3 + 6x^2$

8) $6x^3 - x^2 + 2x + 4$

9) $-9x^3 + 2x^2 + 5x$

10) $5x^4 - 2x^3 + 7x^2$

11) $6x^4 + 5x^3 - 3x^2$

12) $x^2 - 7x + 12$

13) $x^2 - x - 20$

14) $x^2 - 9x + 18$

15) $2x^2 + 21x + 40$

16) $3x^2 + 4x - 32$

17) $-10x^4 + 2x^3 - 8x^2 + 5x$

18) $-12x^3 - x^2 + 33$

19) $4x^3 + 3x^2 - 15x$

20) $-3x^3 - x^2 + 12$

21) $2x^5 - 2x^3 + 8x^2$

22) $3x^3 - 1$

Adding and Subtracting Polynomials

1) $2x^2 + 1$

2) $4x^2 - 9$

3) $3x^2 - 6$

4) $4x^3 + 5x^2 - 8x$

5) $-3x^3 + 3x - 2$

6) $7x^3 + 8$

7) $11x^3 - 4$

8) $x^3 + 5x^2 - 6$

9) $3x$

10) $9x^2 + x - 2$

11) $9x^4 - 8x$

12) $-13x^3 - 4x$

13) $8x^3 - 14x^2 + 3x$

14) $-4x^3 + 14x^2 - 6$

15) $2x^4 + 11x^3$

16) $-6x^3 + 3x$

17) $-13x^4 + 5x$

18) $-7x^4 + 8x$

19) $14x^3 - 4x^2 - 7$

20) $-5x^4 + 12x^3$

Multiplying Monomials

1) $4x^{10}$

2) $36y^5$

3) $-24z^{11}$

4) $40x^6y^4$

5) $-18x^6y^{11}$

6) $21a^{12}b^3$

7) $15x^4y^9$

8) $-30p^6q^8$

9) $48s^9t^9$

10) $-32x^{11}y^5$

11) $27xy^{10}z^3$

12) $24x^{13}y^5$

13) $-28p^5q^{13}$

14) $-45s^5t^7$

15) $-40p^7q^{11}$

16) $-35p^3q^9r^4$

17) $36a^{11}b^8c^4$

18) $-35u^{17}v^{16}$

19) $-20u^5v^{17}z^3$

20) $-18x^4y^4z^{12}$

21) $-42x^6y^5z^6$

22) $28a^{11}b^{13}c^{21}$

Multiplying and Dividing Monomials

1) $6x^7$

2) $12x^9$

3) $-14x^{14}$

4) $-35x^{13}y^{15}$

5) $24x^7y^{11}$

6) $56y^6x^5$

7) $8x^4y^4$

8) $18x^{15}y^{12}$

9) $30x^{12}y^7$

10) $-56x^{12}y^4$

11) $54x^{13}y^6$

12) $48x^{14}y^9$

13) $-35x^{15}y^{17}$

14) $30x^5y^7$

15) $36x^{12}y^{21}$

16) $-20x^{21}y^{13}$

17) $6x^4y$

18) $3x^2y^5$

19) $4x^3y^5$

20) $-6x^4y^4$

Multiplying a Polynomial and a Monomial

1) $x^2 - 5x$

2) $2x + 6$

3) $x^2 - 7x$

4) $x^2 + 9x$

5) $2x^2 - 4x$

6) $20x + 15$

7) $12x^2 - 16x$

8) $5x^2 + 2xy$

9) $3x^2 - 6xy$

10) $18x^2 - 24xy$

11) $6x^2 - 16x$

12) $24x^2 - 36xy$

13) $12x^2 - 6xy$

14) $4x^2 - 12xy$

15) $5x^3 + 5xy^2$

16) $6x^3 - 3xy^2$

17) $54x^2 + 18y^2$

18) $-12x^3y + 8xy$

19) $-18x^2 + 15xy - 9$

20) $6x^2 - 24xy - 18$

Multiplying Binomials

1) $x^2 + x - 12$

2) $x^2 + 8x + 15$

3) $x^2 - 13x + 42$

4) $x^2 - 13x + 36$

5) $x^2 - 12x + 35$

6) $x^2 + 8x + 12$

7) $x^2 - 6x - 27$

8) $x^2 - 13x + 40$

9) $x^2 + 10x + 21$

10) $x^2 - 5x - 36$

11) $x^2 + 12x + 36$

12) $x^2 + 14x + 49$

13) $x^2 - x - 56$

14) $x^2 + 18x + 81$

15) $x^2 - 16x + 64$

16) $x^2 - 4x - 45$

17) $2x^2 + 3x - 20$

18) $2x^2 + 12x + 18$

19) $2x^2 + 14x + 20$

20) $4x^2 - 2x - 6$

Factoring Trinomials

1) $(x + 4)(x + 1)$

2) $(x + 3)(x + 2)$

3) $(x - 1)(x - 3)$

4) $(x - 5)(x - 5)$

5) $(x - 8)(x - 5)$

6) $(x + 6)(x + 2)$

7) $(x - 9)(x + 3)$

8) $(x - 8)(x - 6)$

9) $(x + 8)(x + 7)$

10) $(x - 9)(x + 4)$

11) $(x + 6)(x + 6)$

12) $(x + 7)(x + 9)$

13) $(x - 8)(x + 9)$

14) $(x + 9)(x + 9)$

15) $(x - 8)(x - 8)$

16) $(x - 9)(x - 9)$

17) $2(x + 1)(x + 4)$

18) $2(x - 1)(x + 3)$

19) $(2x + 1)(x + 4)$

20) $(2x - 4)(2x + 6)$

Chapter 11: Geometry and Solid Figures

Math Topics that you'll learn in this Chapter:

- ✓ The Pythagorean Theorem
- ✓ Triangles
- ✓ Polygons
- ✓ Circles
- ✓ Trapezoids
- ✓ Cubes
- ✓ Rectangle Prisms
- ✓ Cylinder

The Pythagorean Theorem

✎ *Do the following lengths form a right triangle?*

1) _____

2) _____
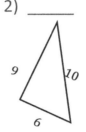

3) _____
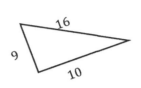

4) _____
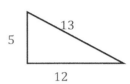

5) _____

6) _____
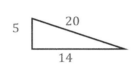

7) _____
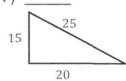

8) _____
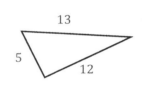

✎ *Find the missing side.*

9) _____
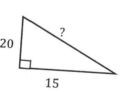

10) _____
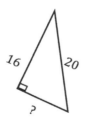

11) _____
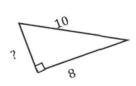

12) _____
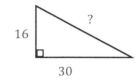

13) _____

14) _____
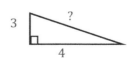

15) _____
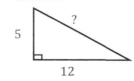

16) _____
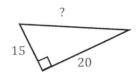

Triangles

✎ **Find the measure of the unknown angle in each triangle.**

1) _____

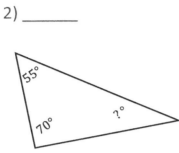

85°
88°
?°

2) _____

55°
70°
?°

3) _____

62°
75°
?°

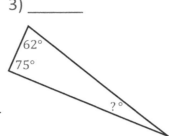

4) _____

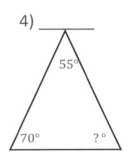

55°
70°
?°

5) _____

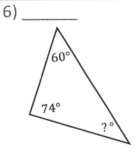

55°
80°
?°

6) _____

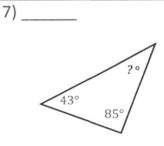

60°
74°
?°

7) _____

?°
43°
85°

8) _____

35°
74° ?°

✎ **Find area of each triangle.**

9) _____

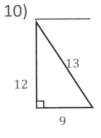

6
11
9

10) _____

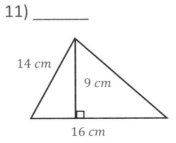

13
12
9

11) _____

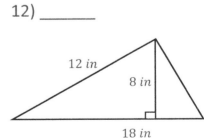

14 cm
9 cm
16 cm

12) _____

12 in
8 in
18 in

Chapter 11: Geometry and Solid Figures

Polygons

✏ *Find the perimeter of each shape.*

1) (square) _____   2) _____   3) _____   4) (square) _____

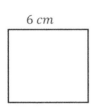

6 cm

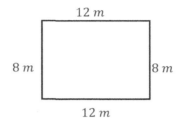

12 m

8 m   8 m

12 m

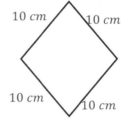

10 cm   10 cm

10 cm   10 cm

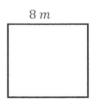

8 m

5) (regular hexagon) _____   6) _____   7) (parallelogram) _____   8) (regular hexagon) _____

16 m

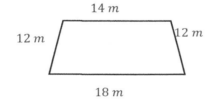

14 m

12 m   12 m

18 m

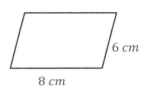

6 cm

8 cm

20 ft

9) _____   10) _____   11) _____   12) (regular hexagon) _____

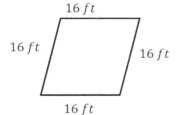

16 ft

16 ft   16 ft

16 ft

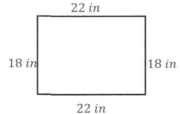

22 in

18 in   18 in

22 in

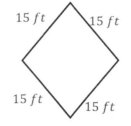

15 ft   15 ft

15 ft   15 ft

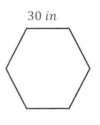

30 in

Circles

✍️ *Find the Circumference of each circle.* (π = 3.14)

1) ____   2) ____   3) ____   4) ____   5) ____   6) ____

     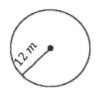 

7) ____   8) ____   9) ____   10) ____   11) ____   12) ____

✍️ *Complete the table below.* (π = 3.14)

	Radius	Diameter	Circumference	Area
Circle 1	2 inches	4 inches	12.56 inches	12.56 square inches
Circle 2		8 meters		
Circle 3				113.04 square feet
Circle 4			50.24 miles	
Circle 5		9 kilometers		
Circle 6	7 centimeters			
Circle 7		18 feet		
Circle 8				78.5 square meters
Circle 9			69.08 inches	
Circle 10	10 feet			

Cubes

✎ *Find the volume of each cube.*

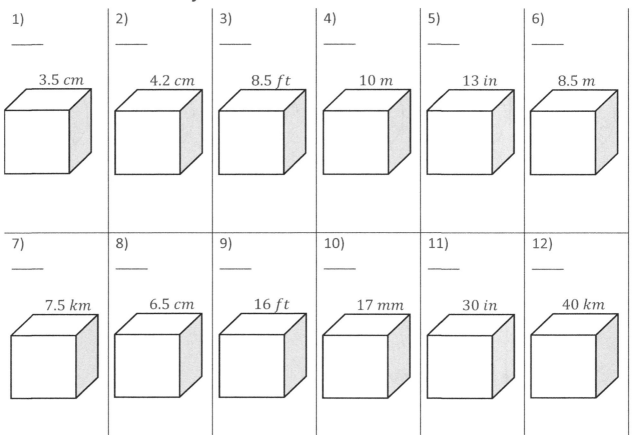

1) ___	2) ___	3) ___	4)	5)	6)
3.5 cm	4.2 cm	8.5 ft	10 m	13 in	8.5 m

7) ___	8)	9)	10)	11)	12)
7.5 km	6.5 cm	16 ft	17 mm	30 in	40 km

✎ *Find the surface area of each cube.*

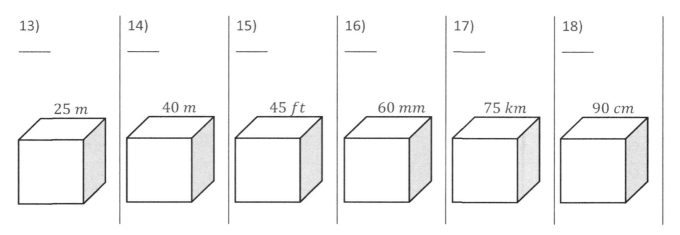

13) ___	14)	15)	16)	17)	18)
25 m	40 m	45 ft	60 mm	75 km	90 cm

Trapezoids

✎ *Find the area of each trapezoid.*

1) _____

12 cm

8 cm

14 cm

2) _____

16 m

12 m

20 m

3) _____

8 ft

6 ft

10 ft

4) _____

9 cm

6 cm

12 cm

5) _____

4 cm

6 cm

12 cm

6) _____

12 in

8 in

16 in

7) _____

20 cm

16 cm

24 cm

8) _____

18 in

14 in

22 in

 Solve.

9) A trapezoid has an area of $78 \ cm^2$ and its height is $10 \ cm$ and one base is $8 \ cm$. What is the other base length? _____

10) If a trapezoid has an area of $160 \ ft^2$ and the lengths of the bases are $12 \ ft$ and $8 \ ft$, find the height. _____

11) If a trapezoid has an area of $180 \ m^2$ and its height is $8 \ m$ and one base is $10 \ m$, find the other base length. _____

12) The area of a trapezoid is $150 \ ft^2$ and its height is $20 \ ft$. If one base of the trapezoid is $12 \ ft$, what is the other base length? _____

Rectangular Prisms

✎ **Find the volume of each Rectangular Prism.**

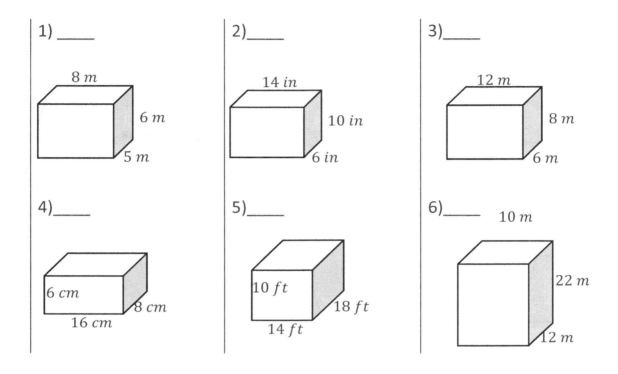

1) _____

8 m
6 m
5 m

2) _____

14 in
10 in
6 in

3) _____

12 m
8 m
6 m

4) _____

6 cm
8 cm
16 cm

5) _____

10 ft
18 ft
14 ft

6) _____

10 m
22 m
12 m

✎ **Find the surface area of each Rectangular Prism.**

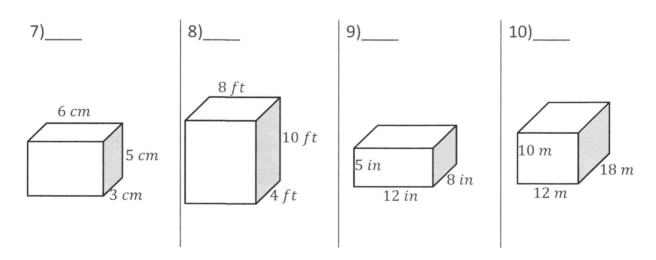

7) _____

6 cm
5 cm
3 cm

8) _____

8 ft
10 ft
4 ft

9) _____

5 in
8 in
12 in

10) _____

10 m
18 m
12 m

Cylinder

✎ *Find the volume of each Cylinder.* (π = 3.14)

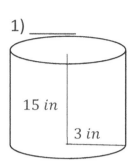

1) _____

15 in

3 in

2) _____

9 cm

5 cm

3) _____

15 in

8 in

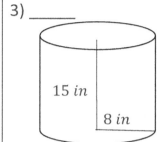

4) _____

18 ft

9 ft

5) _____

18 in

8 in

6) _____

22 in

12 in

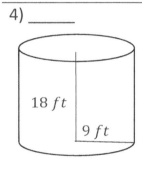
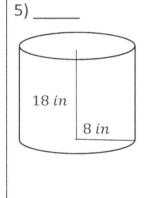
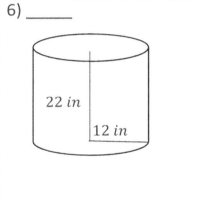

✎ *Find the surface area of each Cylinder.* (π = 3.14)

7) _____

12 in

4 in

8) _____

9 cm

5 cm

9) _____

14 ft

6 ft

10) _____

15 m

5 m

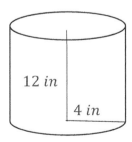
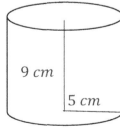
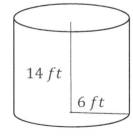
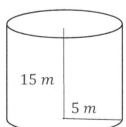

Answers – Chapter 11

The Pythagorean Theorem

1) *no*	7) *yes*	13) 10
2) *no*	8) *yes*	14) 5
3) *no*	9) 25	15) 13
4) *yes*	10) 12	16) 25
5) *no*	11) 6	
6) *no*	12) 34	

Triangles

1) 7°	5) 45°	9) 27
2) 55°	6) 46°	10) 54
3) 43°	7) 52°	11) 72 cm^2
4) 55°	8) 71°	12) 72 in^2

Polygons

1) 24 cm	5) 96 m	9) 64 ft
2) 40 m	6) 56 m	10) 80 in
3) 40 cm	7) 28 cm	11) 60 ft
4) 32 m	8) 120 ft	12) 180 in

Circles

1) $37.68\ in$

2) $62.8\ cm$

3) $119.32\ ft$

4) $75.36\ m$

5) $113.04\ cm$

6) $94.2\ miles$

7) $119.32\ in$

8) $138.16\ ft$

9) $157\ m$

10) $175.84\ m$

11) $219.8\ in$

12) $314\ ft$

	Radius	Diameter	Circumference	Area
Circle 1	2 inches	4 inches	12.56 inches	12.56 square inches
Circle 2	4 meters	8 meters	25.12 meters	50.24 square meters
Circle 3	6 feet	12 feet	37.68 feet	113.04 square feet
Circle 4	8 miles	16 miles	50.24 miles	200.96 square miles
Circle 5	4.5 kilometers	9 kilometers	28.26 kilometers	63.585 square kilometers
Circle 6	7 centimeters	14 centimeters	43.96 centimeters	153.86 square centimeters
Circle 7	9 feet	18 feet	56.52 feet	254.34 square feet
Circle 8	5 meters	10 meters	31.4 meters	78.5 square meters
Circle 9	11 inches	22 inches	69.08 inches	379.94 square inches
Circle 10	10 feet	20 feet	62.8 feet	314 square feet

Cubes

1) $42.875\ cm^3$

2) $74.088\ cm^3$

3) $614.125\ ft^3$

4) $1,000\ m^3$

5) $2,197\ in^3$

6) $614.125\ m^3$

7) $421.875\ km^3$

8) $274.625\ cm^3$

9) $4,096\ ft^3$

10) $4,913\ mm^3$

11) $27,000\ in^3$

12) $64,000\ km^3$

13) $3,750\ m^2$

14) $9,600\ m^2$

15) $12,150\ ft^2$

16) $21,600\ mm^2$

17) $33,750\ km^2$

18) $48,600\ cm^2$

Trapezoids

1) $104 \ cm^2$

2) $216 \ m^2$

3) $54 \ ft^2$

4) $63 \ cm^2$

5) $48 \ cm^2$

6) $112 \ in^2$

7) $352 \ cm^2$

8) $280 \ in^2$

9) $7.6 \ cm$

10) $16 \ ft$

11) $35 \ m$

12) $3 \ ft$

Rectangular Prisms

1) $240 \ m^3$

2) $840 \ in^3$

3) $576 \ m^3$

4) $768 \ cm^3$

5) $2,520 \ ft^3$

6) $2,640 \ m^3$

7) $126 \ cm^2$

8) $304 \ ft^2$

9) $392 \ in^2$

10) $1,032 \ m^2$

Cylinder

1) $423.9 \ in^3$

2) $706.5 \ cm^3$

3) $3,014.4 \ in^3$

4) $4,578.12 \ ft^3$

5) $3,617.28 \ in^3$

6) $9,947.52 \ in^3$

7) $401.92 \ in^2$

8) $439.6 \ cm^2$

9) $753.6 \ ft^2$

10) $628 \ m^2$

Chapter 12: Statistics

Math Topics that you'll learn in this Chapter:

- ✓ Mean, Median, Mode, and Range of the Given Data
- ✓ Pie Graph
- ✓ Probability Problems
- ✓ Permutations and Combinations

117

Mean, Median, Mode, and Range of the Given Data

✏️ *Find the values of the Given Data.*

1) 5, 12, 2, 2, 6

Mode: _____   Range: _____

Mean: _____   Median: _____

2) 5, 9, 3, 6, 4, 3

Mode: _____   Range: _____

Mean: _____   Median: _____

3) 12, 5, 8, 7, 8

Mode: _____   Range: _____

Mean: _____   Median: _____

4) 9, 7, 12, 7, 3, 4

Mode: _____   Range: _____

Mean: _____   Median: _____

5) 9, 7, 10, 5, 7, 4, 14

Mode: _____   Range: _____

Mean: _____   Median: _____

6) 8, 1, 6, 6, 9, 2, 17

Mode: _____   Range: _____

Mean: _____   Median: _____

7) 14, 5, 2, 7, 10, 7, 8, 13

Mode: _____   Range: _____

Mean: _____   Median: _____

8) 12, 14, 6, 4, 10, 8, 2

Mode: _____   Range: _____

Mean: _____   Median: _____

9) 17, 13, 16, 12, 14, 24

Mode: _____   Range: _____

Mean: _____   Median: _____

10) 18, 15, 10, 8, 4, 7, 8, 18

Mode: _____   Range: _____

Mean: _____   Median: _____

Pie Graph

✎ *The circle graph below shows all Wilson's expenses for last month. Wilson spent* $300 *on his bills last month.*

Answer following questions based on the Pie graph.

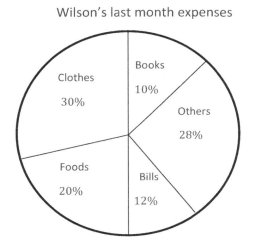

Wilson's last month expenses

1) How much was Wilson's total expenses last month? _____

2) How much did Wilson spend on his clothes last month? _____

3) How much did Wilson spend for foods last month? _____

4) How much did Wilson spend on his books last month? _____

5) What fraction is Wilson's expenses for his bills and clothes out of his total

   expenses last month? _____

Chapter 12: Statistics

Probability Problems

1) If there are 15 red balls and 30 blue balls in a basket, what is the probability that Oliver will pick out a red ball from the basket? _____

Gender	Under 45	45 or older	Total
Male	12	6	18
Female	5	7	12
Total	17	13	30

2) The table above shows the distribution of age and gender for 30 employees in a company. If one employee is selected at random, what is the probability that the employee selected be either a female under age 45 or a male age 45 or older? _____

3) A number is chosen at random from 1 to 18. Find the probability of not selecting a composite number. (A composite number is a number that is divisible by itself, 1 and at least one other whole number) _____

4) There are 6 blue marbles, 8 red marbles, and 5 yellow marbles in a box. If Ava randomly selects a marble from the box, what is the probability of selecting a red or yellow marble? _____

5) A bag contains 20 balls: three green, six black, eight blue, a brown, a red and one white. If 19 balls are removed from the bag at random, what is the probability that a brown ball has been removed? _____

6) There are only red and blue marbles in a box. The probability of choosing a red marble in the box at random is one third. If there are 160 blue marbles, how many marbles are in the box? _____

Chapter 12: Statistics

Permutations and Combinations

✍ *Calculate the value of each.*

1) $5! = $ ____

2) $6! = $ ____

3) $8! = $ ____

4) $5! + 6! = $ ____

5) $8! + 3! = $ ____

6) $6! + 7! = $ ____

7) $8! + 4! = $ ____

8) $9! - 3! = $ ____

✍ *Solve each word problems.*

9) Sophia is baking cookies. She uses milk, flour and eggs. How many different orders of ingredients can she try? _____

10) William is planning for his vacation. He wants to go to restaurant, watch a movie, go to the beach, and play basketball. How many different ways of ordering are there for him? _____

11) How many 7 −digit numbers can be named using the digits $1, 2, 3, 4, 5, 6$ and 7 without repetition? _____

12) In how many ways can 9 boys be arranged in a straight line? _____

13) In how many ways can 8 athletes be arranged in a straight line? _____

14) A professor is going to arrange her 6 students in a straight line. In how many ways can she do this? _____

15) How many code symbols can be formed with the letters for the word BLUE? _____

16) In how many ways a team of 8 basketball players can choose a captain and co-captain? _____

Answers – Chapter 12

Mean, Median, Mode, and Range of the Given Data

1) Mode: 2   Range: 10   Mean: 5.4   Median: 5

2) Mode: 3   Range: 6   Mean: 5   Median: 4.5

3) Mode: 8   Range: 7   Mean: 8   Median: 8

4) Mode: 7   Range: 9   Mean: 7   Median: 7

5) Mode: 7   Range: 10   Mean: 8   Median: 7

6) Mode: 6   Range: 16   Mean: 7   Median: 6

7) Mode: 7   Range: 12   Mean: 8.25   Median: 7.5

8) Mode: *no mode* Range: 12   Mean: 8   Median: 8

9) Mode: *no mode* Range: 12   Mean: 16   Median: 15

10) Mode: 8,18   Range: 14   Mean: 11   Median: 9

Pie Graph

1) $2,500

2) $750

3) $500

4) $250

5) $\frac{21}{50}$

Probability Problems

1) $\frac{1}{3}$

2) $\frac{11}{30}$

3) $\frac{7}{18}$

4) $\frac{13}{19}$

5) $\frac{19}{20}$

6) 240

Permutations and Combinations

1) 120

2) 720

3) 40,320

4) 840

5) 40,326

6) 5,760

7) 40,344

8) 362,874

9) 6

10) 24

11) 5,040

12) 362,880

13) 40,320

14) 720

15) 24

16) 56

Chapter 13:
Functions Operations

Math Topics that you'll learn in this Chapter:

- ✓ Function Notation and Evaluation
- ✓ Adding and Subtracting Functions
- ✓ Multiplying and Dividing Functions
- ✓ Composition of Functions

125

Function Notation and Evaluation

✎ *Evaluate each function.*

1) $f(x) = x - 3$, find $f(-2)$

_____

2) $g(x) = x + 5$, find $g(6)$

_____

3) $h(x) = x + 8$, find $h(2)$

_____

4) $f(x) = -x - 7$, find $f(5)$

_____

5) $f(x) = 2x - 7$, find $f(-1)$

_____

6) $w(x) = -2 - 4x$, find $w(5)$

_____

7) $g(n) = 6n - 3$, find $g(-2)$

_____

8) $h(x) = -8x + 12$, find $h(3)$

_____

9) $k(n) = 14 - 3n$, find $k(3)$

_____

10) $g(x) = 4x - 4$, find $g(-2)$

_____

11) $k(n) = 8n - 7$, find $k(4)$

_____

12) $w(n) = -2n + 14$, find $w(5)$

_____

13) $h(x) = 5x - 18$, find $h(8)$

_____

14) $g(n) = 2n^2 + 2$, find $g(5)$

_____

15) $f(x) = 3x^2 - 13$, find $f(2)$

_____

16) $g(n) = 5n^2 + 7$, find $g(-3)$

_____

17) $h(n) = 5n^2 - 10$, find $h(4)$

_____

18) $g(x) = -3x^2 - 6x$, find $g(2)$

_____

19) $k(n) = 4n^3 + n$, find $k(-5)$

_____

20) $f(x) = -3x + 10$, find $f(3x)$

_____

21) $k(a) = 4a + 9$, find $k(a - 1)$

_____

22) $h(x) = 8x + 4$, find $h(5x)$

_____

Adding and Subtracting Functions

✎ *Perform the indicated operation.*

1) $f(x) = x + 4$

   $g(x) = 2x + 5$

   Find $(f - g)(2)$

   _____

2) $g(x) = x - 2$

   $f(x) = -x - 6$

   Find $(g - f)(-2)$

   _____

3) $h(t) = 4t + 4$

   $g(t) = 3t + 2$

   Find $(h + g)(-1)$

   _____

4) $g(a) = 5a - 7$

   $f(a) = a^2 + 3$

   Find $(g + f)(2)$

   _____

5) $g(x) = 4x - 5$

   $f(x) = 6x^2 + 5$

   Find $(g - f)(-2)$

   _____

6) $h(x) = x^2 + 3$

   $g(x) = -4x + 1$

   Find $(h + g)(4)$

   _____

7) $f(x) = -3x - 9$

   $g(x) = x^2 + 5$

   Find $(f - g)(6)$

   _____

8) $h(n) = -4n^2 + 9$

   $g(n) = 5n + 6$

   Find $(h - g)(5)$

   _____

9) $g(x) = 4x^2 - 3x - 1$

   $f(x) = 6x + 10$

   Find $(g - f)(a)$

   _____

10) $g(t) = -6t - 7$

   $f(t) = -t^2 + 3t + 15$

   Find $(g + f)(t)$

   _____

Multiplying and Dividing Functions

✍ *Perform the indicated operation.*

1) $g(x) = x + 6$

$f(x) = x + 4$

Find $(g.f)(2)$

_____

2) $f(x) = 3x$

$h(x) = -x + 5$

Find $(f.h)(-2)$

_____

3) $g(a) = a + 5$

$h(a) = 2a - 4$

Find $(g.h)(4)$

_____

4) $f(x) = 3x + 2$

$h(x) = 2x - 3$

Find $(\frac{f}{h})(2)$

_____

5) $f(x) = a^2 - 2$

$g(x) = -4 + 3a$

Find $(\frac{f}{g})(2)$

_____

6) $g(a) = 4a + 6$

$f(a) = 2a - 8$

Find $(\frac{g}{f})(3)$

_____

7) $g(t) = t^2 + 6$

$h(t) = 2t - 3$

Find $(g.h)(-3)$

_____

8) $g(x) = x^2 + 3x + 4$

$h(x) = 2x + 6$

Find $(g.h)(2)$

_____

9) $g(a) = 2a^2 - 5a + 1$

$f(a) = 2a^3 - 6$

Find $(\frac{g}{f})(4)$

_____

10) $g(x) = -3x^2 + 4 - 2x$

$f(x) = x^2 - 5$

Find $(g.f)(3)$

_____

Composition of Functions

✍ **Using $f(x) = x + 6$ and $g(x) = 3x$, find:**

1) $f\big(g(1)\big) = $ ____

2) $f\big(g(-1)\big) = $ ____

3) $g\big(f(-3)\big) = $ ____

4) $g\big(f(4)\big) = $ ____

5) $f\big(g(2)\big) = $ ____

6) $g\big(f(3)\big) = $ ____

✍ **Using $f(x) = 2x + 5$ and $g(x) = x - 2$, find:**

7) $g\big(f(2)\big) = $ ____

8) $g\big(f(-2)\big) = $ ____

9) $f\big(g(5)\big) = $ ____

10) $f\big(f(4)\big) = $ ____

11) $g\big(f(3)\big) = $ ____

12) $g\big(f(-3)\big) = $ ____

✍ **Using $f(x) = 4x - 2$ and $g(x) = x - 5$, find:**

13) $g\big(f(-2)\big) = $ ____

14) $f\big(f(4)\big) = $ ____

15) $f\big(g(5)\big) = $ ____

16) $f\big(f(3)\big) = $ ____

17) $g\big(f(-3)\big) = $ ____

18) $g\big(g(6)\big) = $ ____

✍ **Using $f(x) = 6x + 2$ and $g(x) = 2x - 3$, find:**

19) $f\big(g(-3)\big) = $ ____

20) $g\big(f(5)\big) = $ ____

21) $f\big(g(4)\big) = $ ____

22) $f\big(f(3)\big) = $ ____

Answers – Chapter 13

Function Notation and Evaluation

1) -5

2) 11

3) 10

4) -12

5) -9

6) -22

7) -15

8) -12

9) 5

10) -12

11) 25

12) 4

13) 22

14) 52

15) -1

16) 52

17) 70

18) -24

19) -505

20) $-9x + 10$

21) $4a + 5$

22) $40x + 4$

Adding and Subtracting Functions

1) -3

2) 0

3) -1

4) 10

5) -42

6) 4

7) -68

8) -122

9) $4a^2 - 9a - 11$

10) $-t^2 - 3t + 8$

Multiplying and Dividing Functions

1) 48

2) -42

3) 36

4) 8

5) 1

6) -9

7) -135

8) 140

9) $\dfrac{13}{122}$

10) -116

Composition of Functions

1) $f\big(g(1)\big) = 9$

2) $f\big(g(-1)\big) = 3$

3) $g\big(f(-3)\big) = 9$

4) $g\big(f(4)\big) = 30$

5) $f\big(g(2)\big) = 12$

6) $g\big(f(3)\big) = 27$

7) $g\big(f(2)\big) = 7$

8) $g\big(f(-2)\big) = -1$

9) $f\big(g(5)\big) = 11$

10) $f\big(f(4)\big) = 31$

11) $g\big(f(3)\big) = 9$

12) $g\big(f(-3)\big) = -3$

13) $g\big(f(-2)\big) = -15$

14) $f\big(f(4)\big) = 54$

15) $f\big(g(5)\big) = -2$

16) $f\big(f(3)\big) = 38$

17) $g\big(f(-3)\big) = -19$

18) $g\big(g(6)\big) = -4$

19) $f\big(g(-3)\big) = -52$

20) $g\big(f(5)\big) = 61$

21) $f\big(g(4)\big) = 32$

22) $f\big(f(3)\big) = 122$

Time to Test

Time to refine your Math skill with a practice test

In this section, there are two complete CBEST Math Tests. Take these tests to simulate the test day experience. After you've finished, score your test using the answer keys.

Before You Start

-   You'll need a pencil, scratch papers, and a timer to take the test.
-   For each question, there are five possible answers. Choose which one is best.
-   It's okay to guess. There is no penalty for wrong answers.
-   After you've finished the test, review the answer key to see where you went wrong.

Good Luck!

CBEST Mathematics Practice Test 1

2023

Total number of questions: 50

Total time (Calculator): 90 Minutes

Calculators are prohibited for the CBEST exam.

133

Formula Sheet

Perimeter / Circumference

Rectangle

$Perimeter = 2(length) + 2(width)$

Circle

$Circumference = 2\pi(radius)$

Area

Circle

$Area = \pi(radius)^2$

Triangle

$Area = \frac{1}{2}(base)(height)$

Parallelogram

$Area = (base)(height)$

Trapezoid

$Area = \frac{1}{2}(base_1 + base_2)(height)$

Volume

Prism/Cylinder

$Volume = (area\ of\ the\ base)(height)$

Pyramid/Cone

$Volume = \frac{1}{3}(area\ of\ the\ base)(height)$

Sphere

$Volume = \frac{4}{3}\pi(radius)^3$

Length

1 foot = 12 inches

1 yard = 3 feet

1 mile = 5,280 feet

1 meter = 1,000 millimeters

1 meter = 100 centimeters

1 kilometer = 1,000 meters

1 mile ≈ 1.6 kilometers

1 inch = 2.54 centimeters

1 foot ≈ 0.3 meter

Capacity / Volume

1 cup = 8 fluid ounces

1 pint = 2 cups

1 quart = 2 pints

1 gallon = 4 quarts

1 gallon = 231 cubic inches

1 liter = 1,000 milliliters

1 liter ≈ 0.264 gallon

Weight

1 pound = 16 ounces

1 ton = 2,000 pounds

1 gram = 1,000 milligrams

1 kilogram = 1,000 grams

1 kilogram ≈ 2.2 pounds

1 ounce ≈ 28.3 grams

1) The capacity of a red box is 20% bigger than the capacity of a blue box. If the red box can hold 30 equal sized books, how many of the same books can the blue box hold?

   A. 9

   B. 15

   C. 21

   D. 25

   E. 30

2) Kim spent $35 for pants. This was $10 less than triple what she spent for a shirt. How much was the shirt?

   A. $11

   B. $13

   C. $15

   D. $17

   E. $21

3) What is the greatest integer less than $-\frac{32}{5}$?

   A. 0

   B. -2

   C. -4

   D. -6

   E. -7

4) The measure of the angles of a triangle are in the ratio $1:3:5$. What is the measure of the largest angle?

   A. $20°$

   B. $45°$

   C. $85°$

   D. $100°$

   E. $180°$

5) In the figure below, line A is parallel to line B. what is the value of x?

   A. 28

   B. 46

   C. 50

   D. 55

   E. 65

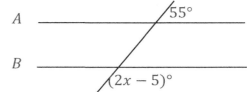

6) In the infinitely repeating decimal below, 1 is the first digit in the repeating pattern. What is the $68th$ digit? $\frac{1}{7} = 0.\overline{142857}$

    A. 1
    B. 2
    C. 4
    D. 5
    E. 7

7) In the following figure, $ABCD$ is a rectangle. If $a = \sqrt{3}$, and $b = 2a$, find the area of the shaded region. (the shaded region is a trapezoid)

    A. $2\sqrt{3}$
    B. $3\sqrt{3}$
    C. $4\sqrt{3}$
    D. $6\sqrt{3}$
    E. $8\sqrt{3}$

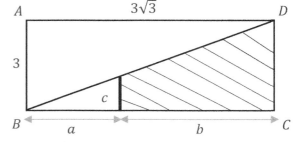

8) The supplement angle of a 45° angle is:

    A. 135°
    B. 105°
    C. 90°
    D. 35°
    E. 15°

9) Anna opened an account with a deposit of $3,000. This account earns 5% simple interest annually. How many years will it take her to earn $600 on her $3,000 deposit?

    A. 2
    B. 4
    C. 5
    D. 6
    E. 8

10) A list of consecutive integers begins with k and ends with n. If $n - k = 46$, how many integers are in the list?

    A. 23
    B. 38
    C. 46
    D. 47
    E. 58

11) Tom picked $2\frac{2}{5}$ baskets of apples, and Sam picked $1\frac{3}{4}$ baskets of apples. How many baskets total did they pick?

    A. $1\frac{2}{3}$

    B. $2\frac{1}{12}$

    C. $3\frac{20}{23}$

    D. $4\frac{3}{20}$

    E. $5\frac{1}{12}$

12) A piece of paper that is $2\frac{3}{5}$ feet long is cut into 2 pieces of different lengths. The shorter piece has a length of x feet. Which inequality expresses all possible values of x?

    A. $x < 2\frac{1}{10}$

    B. $x > 2$

    C. $x < 2\frac{3}{5}$

    D. $x > 1\frac{3}{10}$

    E. $x < 1\frac{3}{10}$

13) In an academy, course grades range from 0 to 100. Anna took 5 courses and her mean course grade was 80. William took 8 courses. If both students have the same sum of course grades, what was William's mean?

    A. 50

    B. 65

    C. 70

    D. 80

    E. 85

14) The set S consists of all odd numbers greater than 5 and less than 30. What is the mean of the numbers in S?

    A. 11

    B. 13

    C. 17

    D. 18

    E. 23

15) In a group of 45 student, 60% can't swim. How many students can swim?

    A. 13

    B. 18

    C. 22

    D. 23

    E. 35

16) $8,400 are distributed equally among 14 person. How much money will each person get?

    A. $400

    B. $450

    C. $584

    D. $600

    E. $800

17) A box contains 6 green sticks, 4 blue sticks, and 2 yellow sticks. Emma picks one without looking. What is the probability that the stick will be green?

    A. $\frac{1}{2}$

    B. $\frac{1}{3}$

    C. $\frac{1}{4}$

    D. $\frac{2}{5}$

    E. $\frac{3}{2}$

18) The price of a Chocolate was raised from $5.40 to $5.67. What was the percent increase in the price?

    A. 4%

    B. 5%

    C. 6%

    D. 8%

    E. 10%

19) In a box of blue and black marbles, the ratio of blue marbles to black marbles is 4: 3. If the box contains 150 black marbles, how many blue marbles are there?

    A. 100

    B. 150

    C. 200

    D. 300

    E. 600

20) $\frac{5}{8}$ of a number is 90. Find the number.

   A. 144

   B. 270

   C. 450

   D. 720

   E. 800

21) A juice mixture contains $\frac{5}{14}$ jar of cherry juice and $\frac{5}{70}$ jar of apple juice. How many jars of cherry juice per jar of apple juice does the mixture contain?

   A. 70

   B. 14

   C. 10

   D. 7

   E. 5

22) The set of possible values of n is $\{5, 3, 7\}$. What is the set of possible values of m if $2m = n + 5$?

   A. $\{2, 4, 7\}$

   B. $\{3, 2, 5\}$

   C. $\{4, 5, 8\}$

   D. $\{5, 4, 6\}$

   E. $\{6, 5, 8\}$

23) If $x = 25$, then which of the following equations are correct?

   A. $x + 10 = 40$

   B. $4x = 100$

   C. $3x = 70$

   D. $\frac{x}{2} = 12$

   E. $\frac{x}{3} = 8$

24) Jack scored a mean of 80 per test in his first 4 tests. In his 5th test, he scored 90. What was Jack's mean score for the 5 tests?

   A. 70

   B. 75

   C. 80

   D. 82

   E. 93

25) The volume of a cube is less than $64\ m^3$. Which of the following can be the cube's side?

A. $2\ m$

B. $4\ m$

C. $8\ m$

D. $10\ m$

E. $11\ m$

26) What is the area of an isosceles right triangle that has one leg that measures $6\ cm$?

A. $16\ cm^2$

B. $18\ cm^2$

C. $24\ cm^2$

D. $32\ cm^2$

E. $36\ cm^2$

27) If $0.00104 = \frac{104}{x}$, what is the value of x?

A. $1,000$

B. $10,000$

C. $100,000$

D. $1,000,000$

E. $10,000,000$

28) A bag is filled with numbered cards from 1 to 15 and picked on at random. What is the probability that the card picked is number 8?

A. $\frac{8}{15}$

B. $\frac{7}{15}$

C. $\frac{5}{15}$

D. $\frac{2}{15}$

E. $\frac{1}{15}$

29) What is the value of x in the figure below?

A. 21

B. 26

C. 36

D. 46

E. 48

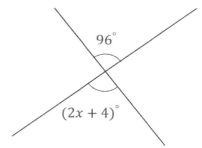

30) How many different two-digit numbers can be formed from the digits 6, 7, and 5, if the numbers must be even and no digit can be repeated?

   A. 1
   B. 2
   C. 3
   D. 4
   E. 5

31) A rectangular concrete driveway is 25 feet long, 6 feet wide, and 24 inches thick. What is the volume of the concrete?

   A. $300\ ft^3$
   B. $600\ ft^3$
   C. $660\ ft^3$
   D. $963\ ft^3$
   E. $1,800\ ft^3$

32) $200(3 + 0.01)^2 - 200 =$

   A. 201.55
   B. 361.08
   C. 702.88
   D. 1,612.02
   E. 1,812.02

33) If $360\ kg$ of vegetables is packed in 90 boxes, how much vegetables will each box contain?

   A. $2.5\ kg$
   B. $3\ kg$
   C. $4\ kg$
   D. $6.5\ kg$
   E. $7\ kg$

34) Each number in a sequence is 4 more than twice the number that comes just before it. If 84 is a number in the sequence, what number comes just before it?

   A. 26
   B. 35
   C. 40
   D. 52
   E. 88

35) $[6 \times (-24) + 8] - (-4) + [4 \times 5] \div 2 = ?$

    A. 148

    B. 132

    C. -122

    D. -136

    E. -144

36) A rectangle has 14 cm wide and 5 cm length. What is the perimeter of this rectangle?

    A. 19 cm

    B. 28 cm

    C. 33 cm

    D. 38 cm

    E. 41 cm

37) What is the value of the following expression? $3\frac{1}{4} + 2\frac{4}{16} + 1\frac{3}{8} + 5\frac{1}{2}$

    A. $3\frac{10}{14}$

    B. $4\frac{1}{2}$

    C. $12\frac{4}{16}$

    D. $12\frac{3}{8}$

    E. $12\frac{4}{8}$

38) A certain insect has a mass of 85 milligrams. What is the insect's mass in grams?

    A. 0.085

    B. 0.08

    C. 0.85

    D. 8.5

    E. 85

39) Removing which of the following numbers will change the average of the numbers to 6?

$$1, 4, 5, 8, 11, 12$$

    A. 1

    B. 4

    C. 5

    D. 8

    E. 11

40) If $m = 6$ and $n = -3$, what is the value of $\frac{5-9(3+n)}{3m-5(2-n)} =$?

    A. $\frac{2}{7}$

    B. $\frac{3}{7}$

    C. $-\frac{4}{7}$

    D. $\frac{5}{7}$

    E. $-\frac{5}{7}$

41) Clara has 28 cookies. She is inviting 7 friends to a party. How many cookies will each friend get?

    A. 2

    B. 4

    C. 7

    D. 8

    E. 21

42) How long will it take to receive \$360 in investment of \$240 at the rate of 10% simple interest?

    A. 9 years

    B. 15 years

    C. 18 years

    D. 21 years

    E. 24 years

43) How many hours are there in 1,800 minutes?

    A. 20 hours

    B. 25 hours

    C. 30 hours

    D. 33 hours

    E. 60 hours

44) What is the value of x in the following equation? $|34 - 78| - x + |-12 + 20| = 36$

    A. 0

    B. 16

    C. 23

    D. 33

    E. 72

45) Mr. Alex wants to fence around a part of his land: (shown below), what is the total length of the fence?

A. 54

B. 56

C. 58

D. 60

E. 62

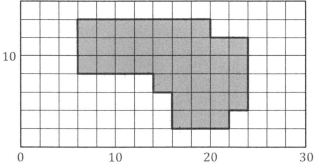

46) According to the following graph, how many more cars did John's sell in 2015 than in 2013

A. 100

B. 200

C. 250

D. 300

D. 400

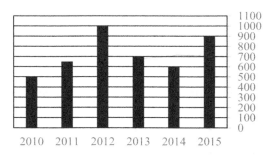

The table below shows the population of a village over five years.

Village	population
1993	1,153
1994	1,434
1995	1,850
1996	2,183
1997	2,923

47) What is the percent increase in population in 1996 compared to 1995?

A. 8%

B. 12%

C. 15%

D. 18%

E. 25%

Use the information below to answer the question.

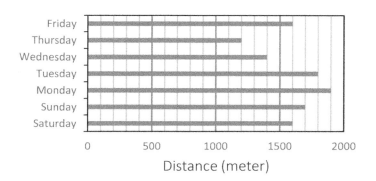

48) The diagram above shows the distance that John run during the week. What is his average distance during the week?

A. 1,300
B. 1,400
C. 1,500
D. 1,600
E. 1,700

Questions 49 to 50 are based on the following data

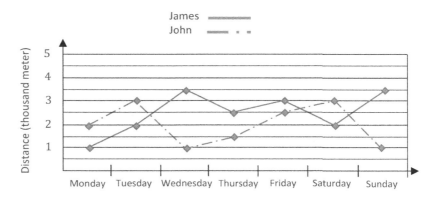

49) The chart above shows the distance James and John run in a week. First, find the average amount of James and John running in a week. What is the difference between the two average values?

   A. 500 meters
   B. 1,000 meters
   C. 1,500 meters
   D. 2,000 meters
   E. 2,500 meters

50) What is the difference between the maximum and minimum distance of James running in a week?

   A. 500 meters
   B. 1,500 meters
   C. 1,000 meters
   D. 2,000 meters
   E. 2,500 meters

End of CBEST Mathematics Practice Test 1

CBEST Mathematics Practice Test 2

2023

Total number of questions: 50

Total time (Calculator): 90 Minutes

Calculators are prohibited for the CBEST exam.

147

Formula Sheet

Perimeter / Circumference

Rectangle
$Perimeter = 2(length) + 2(width)$

Circle
$Circumference = 2\pi(radius)$

Area

Circle
$Area = \pi(radius)^2$

Triangle
$Area = \frac{1}{2}(base)(height)$

Parallelogram
$Area = (base)(height)$

Trapezoid
$Area = \frac{1}{2}(base_1 + base_2)(height)$

Volume

Prism/Cylinder
$Volume = (area\ of\ the\ base)(height)$

Pyramid/Cone
$Volume = \frac{1}{3}(area\ of\ the\ base)(height)$

Sphere
$Volume = \frac{4}{3}\pi(radius)^3$

Length

1 foot = 12 inches

1 yard = 3 feet

1 mile = 5,280 feet

1 meter = 1,000 millimeters

1 meter = 100 centimeters

1 kilometer = 1,000 meters

1 mile $\approx$ 1.6 kilometers

1 inch = 2.54 centimeters

1 foot $\approx$ 0.3 meter

Capacity / Volume

1 cup = 8 fluid ounces

1 pint = 2 cups

1 quart = 2 pints

1 gallon = 4 quarts

1 gallon = 231 cubic inches

1 liter = 1,000 milliliters

1 liter $\approx$ 0.264 gallon

Weight

1 pound = 16 ounces

1 ton = 2,000 pounds

1 gram = 1,000 milligrams

1 kilogram = 1,000 grams

1 kilogram $\approx$ 2.2 pounds

1 ounce $\approx$ 28.3 grams

1) A shoe originally priced at $45.00 was on sale for 15% off. Nick received a 20% employee discount applied to the sale price. How much did Nick pay for the shoes?

   A. $30.60
   B. $34.50
   C. $37.30
   D. $38.25
   E. $42.25

2) Which of the following values when entered in the box will satisfy the statement below?

$$\frac{5}{8} < \square < \frac{4}{5}$$

   A. $\frac{2}{5}$
   B. $\frac{3}{4}$
   C. $\frac{6}{10}$
   D. $\frac{3}{5}$
   E. $\frac{7}{8}$

3) What is the probability a D on of spinning the spinner?

   A. $\frac{1}{5}$
   B. $\frac{1}{10}$
   C. $\frac{3}{10}$
   D. $\frac{2}{5}$
   E. $\frac{3}{10}$

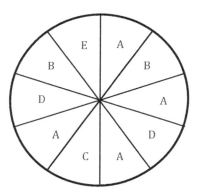

4) Which of the following is a factor of 45?

   A. 7
   B. 9
   C. 11
   D. 13
   E. 14

5) By what percent did the price of a shirt increase if its price was increased from \$15.30 to \$18.36?

    A. 10%

    B. 12%

    C. 16%

    D. 20%

    E. 22%

6) The greatest common factor of 32 and x is 8. How many possible values for x are greater than 10 and less than 60?

    A. 1

    B. 4

    C. 6

    D. 7

    E. 9

7) A box contains 6 strawberry candies, 4 orange candies, and 3 banana candies. If Roberto selects 2 candies at random from this box, without replacement, what is the probability that both candies are not orange?

    A. $\frac{1}{28}$

    B. $\frac{2}{13}$

    C. $\frac{6}{13}$

    D. $\frac{1}{3}$

    E. $\frac{2}{3}$

8) How many integers are between $\frac{7}{2}$ and $\frac{30}{4}$?

    A. 3

    B. 4

    C. 6

    D. 10

    E. 12

9) In a certain state, the sales tax rate increased from 8% to 8.5%. What was the increase in the sales tax on a \$250 item?

    A. \$0.5

    B. \$1.00

    C. \$1.25

    D. \$1.90

    E. \$2.30

10) Triangle ABC is graphed on a coordinate grid with vertices at $A(-3, -2)$, $B(-1, 4)$ and $C(7, 9)$. Triangle ABC is reflected over x axes to create triangle $A'B'C'$. Which order pair represents the coordinate of C'?

    A. $(-7, -9)$

    B. $(-7, 9)$

    C. $(7, -9)$

    D. $(7, 9)$

    E. $(9, 7)$

11) Made a list of all possible products of 2 different numbers in the set below. What fraction of the products are odd?

$$\{1, 4, 6, 5, 7\}$$

    A. $\dfrac{2}{5}$

    B. $\dfrac{3}{10}$

    C. $\dfrac{7}{10}$

    D. $\dfrac{4}{15}$

    E. $\dfrac{8}{17}$

12) If $5n$ is a positive even number, how many odd numbers are in the range from $5n$ up to and including $5n + 6$?

    A. 1

    B. 2

    C. 3

    D. 4

    E. 5

13) If the actual Height of the building is 2,760 centimeters, then what is the scale of the diagram of the building?

    A. $1\ unit = 552\ centimeter$

    B. $1\ unit = 650\ centimeter$

    C. $1\ unit = 680\ centimeter$

    D. $1\ unit = 690\ centimeter$

    E. $1\ unit = 700\ centimeter$

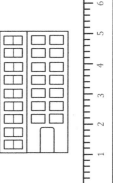

14) If $b = 2$ and $\frac{a}{4} = b$, what is the value of $a^2 + 4b$?

   A. 54

   B. 66

   C. 72

   D. 76

   E. 81

15) Which percentage is closest in value to 0.0099?

   A. 0.1%

   B. 1%

   C. 2%

   D. 9%

   E. 100%

16) What is the surface area of the cylinder below?

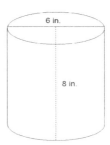

   A. $48\pi\ in^2$

   B. $57\pi\ in^2$

   C. $66\pi\ in^2$

   D. $288\pi\ in^2$

   E. $400\pi\ in^2$

17) A train travels 1,500 miles from New York to Oklahoma. The train covers the first 280 miles in 4 hours. If the train continues to travel at this rate, how many more hours will it take to reach Oklahoma City? Round your answer to the nearest whole hour.

   A. 12

   B. 15

   C. 17

   D. 20

   E. 22

18) The sales price of a laptop is $1,912.50, which is 15% off the original price. What is the original price of the laptop?

   A. $2,750

   B. $2,250

   C. $1,625.625

   D. $956.25

   E. $286.875

19) In a scale diagram, 0.15 inch represents 150 feet. How many inches represent 2.5 $feet$?

    A. 0.001 in

    B. 0.002 in

    C. 0.0025 in

    D. 0.01 in

    E. 0.012 in

20) If $\frac{3}{7}$ of Z is 54, what is $\frac{2}{5}$ of Z?

    A. 44.2

    B. 46.3

    C. 48.4

    D. 50.4

    E. 60.6

21) A car travels at a speed of 72 miles per hour. How far will it travel in 8 hours?

    A. 576

    B. 540

    C. 480

    D. 432

    E. 272

22) If Sam spent $60 on sweets and he spent 25% of the selling price for the tip, how much did he spend?

    A. $66

    B. $69

    C. $72

    D. $75

    E. $77

23) Which of the following numbers has factors that include the smallest factor (other than 1) of 95?

    A. 25

    B. 28

    C. 32

    D. 39

    E. 45

24) $\frac{4^2+3^2+(-5)^2}{(9+10-11)^2}=?$

    A. $\frac{25}{32}$

    B. $-\frac{25}{32}$

    C. 56

    D. -56

    E. 64

25) Angle A and angle B are supplementary. The measure of angle A is 2 times the measure of angle B. What is the measure of angle A in degrees?

    A. $100°$

    B. $120°$

    C. $140°$

    D. $160°$

    E. $170°$

26) Tomas is 6 feet 8.5 inches tall, and Alex is 5 feet 3 inches tall. What is the difference in height, in inches, between Alex and Tomas?

    A. 2.5

    B. 7.5

    C. 12.5

    D. 17.5

    E. 19.5

27) Yesterday Kylie writes 10% of her homework. Today she writes another 18% of the entire homework. What fraction of the homework is left for her to write?

    A. $\frac{4}{25}$

    B. $\frac{7}{25}$

    C. $\frac{10}{25}$

    D. $\frac{18}{25}$

    E. $\frac{21}{25}$

28) In a box of blue and yellow pens, the ratio of yellow pens to blue pens is $2:3$. If the box contains 9 blue pens, how many yellow pens are there?

    A. 2

    B. 3

    C. 4

    D. 5

    E. 6

29) What decimal is equivalent to $-\frac{6}{9}$?

    A. $-0.\overline{5}$

    B. $-0.\overline{6}$

    C. $-0.\overline{65}$

    D. $-0.\overline{7}$

    E. $-0.\overline{75}$

30) The area of a circle is 81π. What is the diameter of the circle?

    A. 3

    B. 6

    C. 8

    D. 9

    E. 18

31) Five years ago, Amy was three times as old as Mike was. If Mike is 10 years old now, how old is Amy?

    A. 4

    B. 8

    C. 12

    D. 14

    E. 20

32) How many positive even factors of 68 are greater than 26 and less than 60?

    A. 0

    B. 1

    C. 2

    D. 4

    E. 6

33) The ratio of two sides of a parallelogram is $2:3$. If its perimeter is $40\ cm$, find the length of its sides.

    A. $6\ cm, 12\ cm$

    B. $8\ cm, 12\ cm$

    C. $10\ cm, 14\ cm$

    D. $12\ cm, 16\ cm$

    E. $14\ cm, 18\ cm$

34) What is the value of x in the following equation? $\frac{3}{4}(x-2) = 3\left(\frac{1}{6}x - \frac{3}{2}\right)$

    A. $\frac{1}{4}$

    B. $-\frac{3}{4}$

    C. -3

    D. 6

    E. -12

35) If x can be any integer, what is the greatest possible value of the expression $2 - x^2$?

    A. -1

    B. 0

    C. 2

    D. 3

    E. 4

36) A store has a container of handballs: 6 green, 5 blue, 8 white, and 10 yellow. If one ball is picked from the container at random, what is the probability that it will be green?

    A. $\frac{1}{5}$

    B. $\frac{6}{11}$

    C. $\frac{6}{29}$

    D. $\frac{8}{25}$

    E. $\frac{11}{25}$

37) Emma answered 9 out of 45 questions on a test incorrectly. What percentage of the questions did she answer correctly?

    A. 10%

    B. 40%

    C. 68%

    D. 80%

    E. 92%

38) If 30% of a number is 12, what is the number?

    A. 12

    B. 25

    C. 40

    D. 45

    E. 50

39) If Anna multiplies her age by 5 and then adds 3, she will get a number equal to her mother's age. If x is her mother's age, what is Anna's age in terms of x?

    A. $\frac{x-3}{5}$

    B. $\frac{x-5}{3}$

    C. $3x + 5$

    D. $5x - 3$

    E. $x - 3$

40) A line connects the midpoint of AB (point E), with point C in the square $ABCD$. Calculate the area of the acquired trapezoid shape if the square has a side of $4\ m$.

    A. $4\ cm^2$

    B. $12\ cm^2$

    C. $15\ cm^2$

    D. $18\ cm^2$

    E. $24\ cm^2$

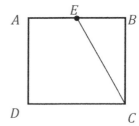

41) Which of the following is between 0.0048 and 0.069 ?

    A. 0.07

    B. 0.0039

    C. 0.091

    D. 0.081

    E. 0.061

42) The reciprocal of $\frac{3}{5}$ is added to the reciprocal of $\frac{1}{4}$. What is the reciprocal of this sum?

    A. $\frac{3}{5}$

    B. $\frac{5}{3}$

    C. $\frac{3}{17}$

    D. $\frac{17}{3}$

    E. $\frac{19}{3}$

43) What is the solution to $\frac{0.02}{0.25} = \frac{1.25}{x}$?

    A. 0.150

    B. 1.156

    C. 11.565

    D. 15.625

    E. 16.625

44) Which of the following numbers is greater than -0.0029 ?

    A. -0.003

    B. -0.029

    C. -0.03

    D. -0.0028

    E. -0.028

45) The weight of a pan is 3 pounds and 8 ounces. What is the weight of 5 pan?

    A. 16 pounds and 6 ounces

    B. 16 pounds and 8 ounces

    C. 17 pounds and 6 ounces

    D. 17 pounds and 8 ounces

    E. 18 pounds and 8 ounces

Use the graph below to answer the question.

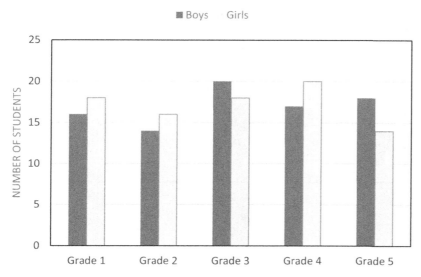

46) According to the chart above, which class has the least number of girl students?

   A. Grade 1
   B. Grade 2
   C. Grade 3
   D. Grade 4
   E. Grade 5

Use the chart below to answer the question.

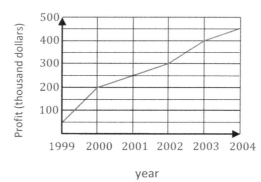

year

47) What is the percent increase for profit from 2001 to 2003?

   A. 60%
   B. 55%
   C. 44%
   D. 40%
   E. 20%

Use the graph below to answer the question.

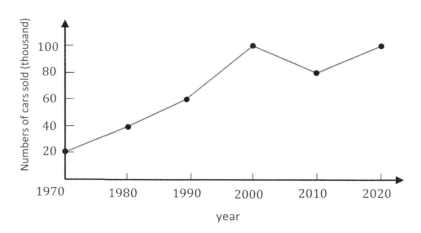

48) The graph shows the number of cars sold by a company over 50 years. Between what years did the number of sales increase by the greatest amount?

    A. Between 1970 and 1980

    B. Between 1980 and 1990

    C. Between 1990 and 2000

    D. Between 2000 and 2010

    E. Between 2010 and 2020

Use the table below to answer the question.

Fruit name	harvest
Orange	200 thousand
Apple	500 thousand
Watermelon	250 thousand
Banana	150 thousand

49) The table above shows Mr. Sullivan's garden harvest. According to the table, what was his total harvest?

    A. 1,100

    B. 11,000

    C. 110,000

    D. 1,100,000

    E. 11,000,000

Use the graphs below to answer the question.

Produced by a car factory

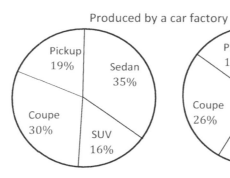

Revenue from sales in 2000
$850,000

Revenue from sales in 2006
$980,000

50) What is the difference between the amount of revenue earned from the sale of SUVs in 2006 compared to 2000?

A. 1,000

B. 3,000

C. 6,000

D. 30,000

E. 60,000

End of CBEST Mathematics Practice Test 2

CBEST Math Practice Tests Answer Keys

Now, it's time to review your results to see where you went wrong and what areas you need to improve.

CBEST Practice Test 1						CBEST Practice Test 2					
1	D	21	E	41	B	1	A	21	A	41	E
2	C	22	D	42	B	2	B	22	D	42	C
3	E	23	B	43	C	3	A	23	E	43	D
4	D	24	D	44	B	4	B	24	A	44	D
5	E	25	A	45	D	5	D	25	B	45	D
6	C	26	B	46	B	6	B	26	D	46	E
7	C	27	C	47	D	7	C	27	D	47	A
8	A	28	E	48	D	8	B	28	E	48	C
9	B	29	D	49	A	9	C	29	B	49	D
10	D	30	B	50	E	10	C	30	E	50	E
11	D	31	A			11	B	31	E		
12	E	32	D			12	C	32	B		
13	A	33	C			13	B	33	B		
14	D	34	C			14	C	34	E		
15	B	35	C			15	A	35	C		
16	D	36	D			16	C	36	C		
17	A	37	D			17	C	37	D		
18	B	38	A			18	B	38	C		
19	C	39	E			19	C	39	A		
20	A	40	E			20	D	40	B		

CBEST Mathematics
Practice Tests Answers and
Explanations

CBEST Mathematics Practice Test 1

Answers and Explanations

1) Choice D is correct

The capacity of a red box is 20% bigger than the capacity of a blue box and it can hold 30 books. Therefore, we want to find a number that 20% bigger than that number is 30. Let x be that number. Then: $1.20 \times x = 30$. Divide both sides of the equation by 1.2. Then: $x = \frac{30}{1.20} = 25$

2) Choice C is correct

Convert everything into an equation: $35 = (3 \times \text{shirt}) - 10$

Now, solve the equation: $45 = 3 \text{ shirt} \rightarrow \text{shirt} = \frac{45}{3} = 15$. The price of the shirt was $15.

3) Choice E is correct

First, convert the improper fraction to a mixed number: $-\frac{32}{5} = -6\frac{2}{5}$

The two closest integers to this fraction are -7 and -6.

The integer less than $-\frac{32}{5}$ is -7.

4) Choice D is correct

Let x equal the smallest angle of the triangle. Then, the three angles are $x, 3x$, and $5x$. The sum of the angles of a triangle is 180. Set up an equation using this to find x:

$x + 3x + 5x = 180 \rightarrow 9x = 180 \rightarrow x = 20$

Since the question asks for the measure of the largest angle, $5x = 5(20) = 100°$

5) Choice E is correct

The angle $(2x - 5)$ and 55 are supplementary angles. Therefore:

$(2x - 5) + 55 = 180 \rightarrow 2x + 50 = 180 \rightarrow 2x = 180 - 50 \rightarrow 2x = 130 \rightarrow x = \frac{130}{2} \rightarrow x = 65$

6) Choice C is correct

There are 6 digits in the repeating decimal (0.142857), so digit 1 would be the first, seventh, thirteenth digit and so on. To find the 68th digit, divide 68 by 6.

$68 \div 6 = 11r2$

7) Choice C is correct

Based on triangle similarity theorem: $\frac{a}{a+b} = \frac{c}{3} \rightarrow c = \frac{3a}{a+b} = \frac{3\sqrt{3}}{3\sqrt{3}} = 1 \rightarrow$ Area of shaded region is:

$\left(\frac{c+3}{2}\right)(b) = \frac{4}{2} \times 2\sqrt{3} = 4\sqrt{3}$

8) Choice A is correct

Two Angles are supplementary when they add up to 180 degrees.

$135° + 45° = 180°$

9) Choice B is correct

Use simple interest formula:

$I = prt$ ($I = interest$, $p = principal$, $r = rate$, $t = time$)

$I = prt \rightarrow 600 = (3,000)(0.05)(t) \rightarrow 600 = 150t \rightarrow t = 4$

10) Choice D is correct

Consider the case where $k = 1$

$n - k = 46 \rightarrow n - 1 = 46 \rightarrow n - 1 + 1 = 46 + 1 \rightarrow n = 47$

The list of integers from 1 to 47 contains 47 numbers.

11) Choice D is correct

To solve, add the two given fractions: $2\frac{2}{5} + 1\frac{3}{4}$

The common denominator is 20: $2\frac{8}{20} + 1\frac{15}{20} = 3\frac{23}{20} = 4\frac{3}{20}$

12) Choice E is correct

The original piece of paper is $2\frac{3}{5}$ feet long.

The shorter piece is x feet long, and it must be less than half the length of the original piece of paper. Since half of $2\frac{3}{5}$ is $1\frac{3}{10}$ it follows that $x < 1\frac{3}{10}$.

13) Choice A is correct

First, find the sum of course grade of Anna, $average = \frac{sum\ of\ terms}{number\ of\ terms} \Rightarrow$

$80 = \frac{sum\ of\ course\ grade}{5} \rightarrow the\ sum\ of\ course\ grade = 80 \times 5 = 400$

Anna and William have the same sum of course grade, now find the Williams mean $average = \frac{sum\ of\ course\ grade}{number\ of\ course} \Rightarrow \frac{400}{8} = 50$

14) Choice D is correct

List in order the odd numbers between 5 to 30: $7, 9, 11, 13, 15, 17, 19, 21, 23, 25, 27$, and 29. Since, the numbers are consecutive odd numbers, the mean and the median are equal. The median is the number in the middle. Since we have 12 numbers, the median is the average of numbers 6 and 7 which are 17 and 19. The mean (or the median) is: Mean $= \frac{17+19}{2} = 18$

15) Choice B is correct

60% of students can't swim→ $100 - 60 = 40\%$ can swim.

Then: $0.40 \times 45 = 18$

16) Choice D is correct

Money received by 14 person = \$8,400. So, the money received by one person is:

$\frac{\$8,400}{14} = \$600$

17) Choice A is correct

There are 12 sticks in the box $(6 + 4 + 2)$. So, the probability that Emma picks a green stick is:
$Probability = \frac{6}{12} = \frac{1}{2}$

18) Choice B is correct

Use the percent increase expression to find the answer:

$\frac{new\ price - original\ price}{original\ price} = \frac{5.67 - 5.40}{5.40} = 0.05 = 5\%$

19) Choice C is correct

Let x be the number of blue marbles. Write the items in the ratio as a fraction:

$\frac{x}{150} = \frac{4}{3} \rightarrow 3x = 600 \rightarrow x = 200$

20) Choice A is correct

Let x be the number: $\frac{5}{8}x = 90 \rightarrow x = 90 \times \frac{8}{5} = \frac{720}{5} = 144$

21) Choice E is correct

Set up a proportion to solve: $\frac{\frac{5}{14}\ cherry}{\frac{5}{70}\ apple} = \frac{x\ cherry}{1\ apple} \rightarrow \frac{5}{14} \times \frac{70}{5} = x \rightarrow x = \frac{70}{14} = \frac{10}{2} \rightarrow x = 5$

22) Choice D is correct

$2m = n + 5 \rightarrow m = \frac{n+5}{2}$. Substitute each value of n to find the values of m:

$m = \frac{5+5}{2} = \frac{10}{2} = 5$

$m = \frac{3+5}{2} = \frac{8}{2} = 4$

$m = \frac{7+5}{2} = \frac{12}{2} = 6$

The set of m is $\{5,4,6\}$.

23) Choice B is correct

Plug in 25 for x in the equation.

A. $x + 10 = 40 \rightarrow 25 + 10 \neq 40$

B. $4x = 100 \rightarrow 4(25) = 100$

C. $3x = 70 \rightarrow 3(25) \neq 70$

D. $\frac{x}{2} = 12 \rightarrow \frac{25}{2} \neq 12$

E. $\frac{x}{3} = 8 \rightarrow \frac{25}{3} \neq 8$

Only choice B is correct.

24) Choice D is correct

Jack scored a mean of 80 per test. In the first 4 tests, the sum of scores is:

$80 \times 4 = 320$. Now, calculate the mean over the 5 tests: $\frac{320+90}{5} = \frac{410}{5} = 82$

25) Choice A is correct

Volume of the cube is less than $64 \ m^3$. Use the formula of volume of cubes.

$Volume = (one \ side)^3 \Rightarrow 64 = (one \ side)^3$. Find the cube root of both sides.

$64 = (one \ side)^3 \rightarrow one \ side = \sqrt[3]{64} = 4 \ m$

Then: $4 = $ one side. The side of the cube is less than 4. Only choice A is less than 4.

26) Choice B is correct

First draw an isosceles triangle. Remember that two legs of the triangle are equal.

Let put a for the legs. Then:

$a = 6 \Rightarrow$ Area of the triangle is $= \frac{1}{2}(6 \times 6) = \frac{36}{2} = 18 \ cm^2$ $\qquad a$

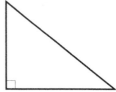

27) Choice C is correct

Solve for x: $0.00104 = \frac{104}{x}$, multiply both sides by x, $(0.00104)(x) = \frac{104}{x}(x)$. $\quad a$

Simplify: $0.00104x = 104$. Divide both side by 0.00104: $\frac{0.00104x}{0.00104} = \frac{104}{0.00104}$, simplify

$x = \frac{104}{0.00104} = 100,000$

28) Choice E is correct

The number of cards in the bag is 15.

$Probability = \frac{number \ of \ desired \ outcomes}{number \ of \ total \ outcomes} = \frac{1}{15}$

29) Choice D is correct

$(2x + 4)°$ and $96°$ are vertical angles. Vertical angles are equal in measure.

Then: $2x + 4 = 96 \rightarrow 2x = 92 \rightarrow x = 46$

30) Choice B is correct

The two-digit numbers must be even, so the only possible two-digit numbers must end in 6, since 6 is the only even digit given in the problem. Since the numbers cannot be repeated, the only possibilities for two-digit even numbers are 76 and 56. Thus, the answer is two possible two-digit numbers.

31) Choice A is correct

First convert 24 inches to feet. 12 inch $= 1$ feet, thus: $24 \div 12 = 2\ feet$. Then, calculate the volume, in cubic feet: $25 \times 6 \times 2 = 300\ ft^3$

32) Choice D is correct

First calculate exponents value, then multiplying and subtracting:

$200(3 + 0.01)^2 - 200 = 200(3.01)^2 - 200 = 200(9.0601) - 200 = 1,612.02$

33) Choice C is correct

Since 90 boxes contain $360\ kg$ vegetable. Therefore, 1 box contains $\frac{360\ kg}{90} = 4\ kg$ vegetable.

34) Choice C is correct

Let n represent a number in the sequence, and let x represent the number that comes just before n. $n = 4 + 2x \rightarrow 84 = 4 + 2x \rightarrow 80 = 2x \rightarrow x = 40$

35) Choice C is correct

Use PEMDAS (order of operation): $[6 \times (-24) + 8] - (-4) + [4 \times 5] \div 2 =$

$[-144 + 8] - (-4) + [20] \div 2 = [-144 + 8] + 4 + 10 = [-136] + 4 + 10 = -122$

36) Choice D is correct

Perimeter of rectangle is equal to the sum of all the sides of the rectangle:

Perimeter $= 2(14) + 2(5) = 28 + 10 = 38\ cm$

37) Choice D is correct

$3\frac{1}{4} + 2\frac{4}{16} + 1\frac{3}{8} + 5\frac{1}{2}$. Convert all the fractions to a common denominator (16):

$3\frac{4}{16} + 2\frac{4}{16} + 1\frac{6}{16} + 5\frac{8}{16} = (3 + 2 + 1 + 5) + \left(\frac{4+4+6+8}{16}\right) = 11 + 1\frac{6}{16} = 12\frac{6}{16} = 12\frac{3}{8}$

38) Choice A is correct

One gram is equal to 1,000 milligrams, or 1 milligram is equal to $\frac{1}{1,000}$ gram.

Thus, 85 milligrams $= \frac{85}{1,000} = 0.085$ gram

39) Choice E is correct

Check each choice provided:

A. 1 $\frac{4+5+8+11+12}{5} = \frac{40}{5} = 8$

B. 4 $\frac{1+5+8+11+12}{5} = \frac{37}{5} = 7.4$

C. 5 $\frac{1+4+8+11+12}{5} = \frac{36}{5} = 7.2$

D. 8 $\frac{1+4+5+11+12}{5} = \frac{33}{5} = 6.6$

E. 11 $\frac{1+4+5+8+12}{5} = \frac{30}{5} = 6$

40) Choice E is correct

Substitute 6 for m and -3 for n:

$\frac{5-9(3+n)}{3m-5(2-n)} = \frac{5-9(3+(-3))}{3(6)-5(2-(-3))} = \frac{5-9(0)}{18-5(5)} = \frac{5}{18-25} = \frac{5}{-7} = -\frac{5}{7}$

41) Choice B is correct

To answer this question, we need to divide 28 by 7: $\frac{28}{7} = 4$

42) Choice B is correct

Simple interest (y) is calculated by multiplying the initial deposit (p), by the interest rate (r), and time (t). $360 = 240 \times 0.10 \times t \rightarrow 360 = 24t \rightarrow t = \frac{360}{24} = 15$

So, it takes 15 years to get \$360 with an investment of \$240.

43) Choice C is correct

There are 60 minutes in 1 hour. Divide the number of minutes by the number of minutes in 1 hour: $\frac{1,800}{60} = 30$ hours

44) Choice B is correct

First calculate absolute values: $|-44| - x + |8| = 36 \rightarrow 44 - x + 8 = 36$

Combine like terms: $44 + 8 - 36 = x \rightarrow x = 16$

45) Choice D is correct

According to the figure above, the length of each side of a small square is 2 units. First, count the number of units around the shaded part. The number of sides all around the shaded part is 30. So the total length of the fence needed is $2 \times 30 = 60$.

46) Choice B is correct

$900 - 700 = 200$

47) Choice D is correct

Use the percent increase formula to find the answer:

$Percent\ change = \frac{New\ Value - Old\ Value}{Old\ Value} \times 100\% \Rightarrow \frac{2,183 - 1,850}{1,850} \times 100\% = 18\%$

48) Choice D is correct

$Average = \frac{sum\ of\ data}{number\ of\ data} = \frac{1,600 + 1,200 + 1,400 + 1,800 + 1,900 + 1,700 + 1,600}{7} = \frac{11,200}{7} = 1,600$

49) Choice A is correct

$Average = \frac{sum\ of\ data}{number\ of\ data}$

$James\ Average = \frac{(1,000 + 2,000 + 3,500 + 2,500 + 3,000 + 2,000 + 3,500)}{7} = \frac{17,500}{7} = 2,500\ meter$

$John\ Average = \frac{(2,000 + 3,000 + 1,000 + 1,500 + 2,500 + 3,000 + 1,000)}{7} = \frac{14,000}{7} = 2,000\ meter$

$Difference\ average = James\ Average - John\ Average = 2,500 - 2,000 = 500\ meter$

50) Choice E is correct

Maximum distance James $= 3,500$ meter

Minimum distance James $= 1,000$ meter

$3,500 - 1,000 = 2,500$ meter

CBEST Mathematics Practice Test 2

Answers and Explanations

1) Choice A is correct

First, find the sale price. 15% of $45.00 is $6.75, so the sale price is

$45.00 − $6.75 = $38.25. Next, find the price after Nick's employee discount. 20% × $38.25 = $7.65, so, the final price of the shoes is $38.25 − $7.65 = $30.60.

2) Choice B is correct

Let's compare the fractions by converting them to decimals:

A. $\frac{2}{5} = 0.4$

B. $\frac{3}{4} = 0.75$

C. $\frac{6}{10} = 0.6$

D. $\frac{3}{5} = 0.6$

E. $\frac{7}{8} = 0.875$

Only 0.75 can be entered in the box.

$\frac{5}{8} < \square < \frac{4}{5} \rightarrow 0.625 < \square < 0.8 \rightarrow 0.625 < 0.75 < 0.8$

3) Choice A is correct

The total number of possible sections in the spinner $= 10$

There are two sections containing Number D. Then, the probability of spinning a D is: $\frac{2}{10} = \frac{1}{5}$

4) Choice B is correct

The factors of 45 are: $\{ 1, 3, 5, 9, 15, 45 \}$. Only choice B is correct.

5) Choice D is correct

$Percent\ of\ change = \frac{new\ number - original\ number}{original\ number} = \frac{18.36 - 15.30}{15.30} = 20\%$

6) Choice B is correct

First find the multiples of 8 that fall between 10 and 60: $16, 24, 32, 40, 48, 56$. Since the greatest common factor of 32 and x is 8, x cannot be 32 (otherwise the GCF would be 32, not 8). There are 5 remaining values: $16, 24, 40, 48$ and 56. Number 16 is also not possible (otherwise the GCF would be 16, not 8). Then, there are 4 possible values for x.

7) Choice C is correct

The total number of candies in the box is $6 + 4 + 3 = 13$. The number of candies that are not orange is $6 + 3 = 9$. The probability of the first candy not being orange is $\frac{9}{13}$. Now, out of 12 candies, there are 8 candies left that are not orange. The probability of the second candy not being orange is $\frac{8}{12}$. Multiply these two probabilities to get the solution: $\frac{9}{13} \times \frac{8}{12} = \frac{72}{156} = \frac{24}{52} = \frac{6}{13}$

8) Choice B is correct

First, change the improper fractions into mixed numbers: $\frac{7}{2} = 3\frac{1}{2}$ and $\frac{30}{4} = 7\frac{1}{2}$

The integers between these two values are $4, 5, 6$ and 7. So, there are 4 integers between $\frac{7}{5}$ and $\frac{30}{4}$.

9) Choice C is correct

The increase in sales tax percentage is $8.5\% - 8.0\% = 0.5\%$

0.5% of \$250 is $(0.5\%)(250) = (0.005)(250) = 1.25\$$

10) Choice C is correct

When a point is reflected over x axes, the (y) coordinate of that point changes to $(-y)$ while its x coordinate remains the same. $C(7, 9) \rightarrow C'(7, -9)$

11) Choice B is correct

First, list the products:

$1 \times 4 = 4$

$1 \times 6 = 6$

$1 \times 5 = 5$

$1 \times 7 = 7$

$4 \times 6 = 24$

$4 \times 5 = 20$

$4 \times 7 = 28$

$6 \times 5 = 30$

$6 \times 7 = 42$

$5 \times 7 = 35$

Out of 10 results, 3 numbers are odd. The answer is: $\frac{3}{10}$

12) Choice C is correct

Since $5n$ is even, then $5n + 1$ must be odd. Thus $5n + 3$ and $5n + 5$ are also odd. So, there are a total of 3 numbers in this range that are odd.

13) Choice B is correct

The height of the building is 4 units.

$2,760 \; centimeters \div 4 = 690 \; centimeters$

14) Choice C is correct

First, use the given information to calculate the value of a: $\frac{a}{4} = b \rightarrow \frac{a}{4} = 2 \rightarrow a = 8$

Now, calculate $a^2 + 4b$ by substituting $a = 8$ and $b = 2$, $\quad (8)^2 + 4(2) = 72$

15) Choice A is correct

Since 0.0099 is equal to 0.99%, the closest to that value is 0.1%.

16) Choice C is correct

Surface Area of a cylinder $= 2\pi r(r + h)$, The radius of the cylinder is 3 $(6 \div 2)$ inches and its height is 8 inches.

Therefore, Surface Area of a cylinder $= 2\pi(3)(3 + 8) = 66\pi \; in^2$

17) Choice C is correct

First, find the speed of the train in miles per hour: $280 \div 4 = 70$ miles per hour

The number of miles left to travel is: $1,500 - 280 = 1,220$ miles

To find the number of hours left, use the equation

$d = rt \rightarrow (distance) = (rate) \times (time) \rightarrow 1,220 = 70t$

$t = \frac{1,220}{70} = 17.4285714$ hours. That number rounded to the nearest whole hour is 17 hours.

18) Choice B is correct

Let x be the original price. Then:

$$\$1,912.50 = x - 0.15(x) \rightarrow 1,912.50 = 0.85x \rightarrow x = \frac{1,912.50}{0.85} \rightarrow x = 2,250$$

19) Choice C is correct

Let x be the number of inches representing 2.5 feet. Set up a proportion and solve for x: $\frac{x}{2.5} = \frac{0.15}{150} \rightarrow x = \frac{0.15 \times 2.5}{150} \rightarrow x = 0.0025 \; in$

20) Choice D is correct

Set an equation: $\frac{3}{7}Z = 54$

Solve for $Z: \rightarrow Z = 54 \times \frac{7}{3} = 126,$ then, calculate $\frac{2}{5}Z : \frac{2}{5} \times 126 = 50.4$

21) Choice A is correct

To answer this question, multiply 72 miles per hour to $8 \rightarrow 72 \times 8 = 576$ miles

22) Choice D is correct

The spent amount is \$60, and the tip is 25%. Then: $tip = 0.25 \times 60 = \$15$

Final price = Selling price+tip $\rightarrow$ final price = \$60 + \$15 = \$75

23) Choice E is correct

To find the smallest factor of 95, list the factors: $1, 5, 19,$ and $95.$ The smallest factor (other than 1) is 5. Of the choices listed $(28, 32, 39,$ and $45)$, only 45 is a multiple of 5.

24) Choice A is correct

Adding exponents is done by calculating each exponent first and then adding and dividing:

$$\frac{4^2 + 3^2 + (-5)^2}{(9 + 10 - 11)^2} = \frac{16 + 9 + 25}{(8)^2} = \frac{50}{64} = \frac{25}{32}$$

25) Choice B is correct

Angle A and angle B are supplementary, so the sum of their angles is $180°$.

Let a equal the measure of angle A, and let b equal the measure of angle B.

$a + b = 180$

The measure of angle A is 2 times the measure of angle B.

$$a = 2b \rightarrow 2b + b = 180 \rightarrow 3b = 180 \rightarrow b = \frac{180}{3} = 60$$

$a = 2b = 2(60) = 120$

Therefore, the measure of angle A is $120°$.

26) Choice D is correct

First, convert their heights from feet and inches to inches, by multiplying the number of feet by 12 and adding the inches. Tomas:

6 feet +8.5 inches. 6(12 inches) +8.5 inches = 72 inches +8.5 inches = 80.5 inches

Alex: 5 feet +3 inches. 5(12 inches)+3 inches = 60 inches +3 inches = 63 inches

Then, subtract Alex's height from Tomas's height: $80.5 - 63 = 17.5$

27) Choice D is correct

So far, Kylie has written $10\% + 18\% = 28\%$ of the entire homework. That means she has $100\% - 28\% = 72\%$ left to write. $72\% = \frac{72}{100} = \frac{18}{25}$

28) Choice E is correct

Let x be the number of yellow pens. Write a proportion and solve: $\frac{yellow}{blue} = \frac{2}{3} = \frac{x}{9}$

Solve the equation: $18 = 3x \rightarrow x = 6$

29) Choice B is correct

To find the decimal equivalent to $-\frac{6}{9}$, divide 6 by 9. Then: $-\frac{6}{9} = -0.66666 \ldots = -0.\overline{6}$

30) Choice E is correct

The formula for the area of the circle is πr^2, The area is 81π. Therefore:

$A = \pi r^2 \Rightarrow 81\pi = \pi r^2$, Divide both sides by π: $81 = r^2 \Rightarrow r = 9$, Diameter of a circle is $2 \times radius$. Then: $Diameter = 2 \times 9 = 18$

31) Choice E is correct

Five years ago, Amy was three times as old as Mike. Mike is 10 years now. Therefore, 5 years ago Mike was 5 years. Five years ago, Amy was: $A = 3 \times 5 = 15$, Now Amy is 20 years old: $15 + 5 = 20$

32) Choice B is correct

List the factors of 68: 1 and 68, 2 and 34, 4 and 17. There is one factor greater than 26 and less than 60.

33) Choice B is correct

Let the lengths of two sides of the parallelogram be $2x\ cm$ and $3x\ cm$ respectively. Then, its perimeter $= 2(2x + 3x) = 10x$

Therefore, $10x = 40 \rightarrow x = 4$

One side $= 2(4) = 8\ cm$ and other side is: $3(4) = 12\ cm$

34) Choice E is correct

Isolate x in the equation and solve. Then:

$\frac{3}{4}(x - 2) = 3\left(\frac{1}{6}x - \frac{3}{2}\right)$, expand $\frac{3}{4}$ and 3 to the parentheses $\rightarrow \frac{3}{4}x - \frac{3}{2} = \frac{1}{2}x - \frac{9}{2}$. Add $\frac{3}{2}$ to both sides: $\frac{3}{4}x - \frac{3}{2} + \frac{3}{2} = \frac{1}{2}x - \frac{9}{2} + \frac{3}{2}$. Simplify: $\frac{3}{4}x = \frac{1}{2}x - 3$. Now, subtract $\frac{1}{2}x$ from both sides: $\frac{3}{4}x - \frac{1}{2}x = \frac{1}{2}x - 3 - \frac{1}{2}x$. Simplify: $\frac{1}{4}x = -3$. Multiply both sides by 4:

$(4)\frac{1}{4}x = -3(4)$, simplify $x = -12$

35) Choice C is correct

To answer this question, assign several positive and negative values to x and determine what the value of the expression will be:

x	-1	0	2	3	4
$2-x^2$	1	2	-2	-7	-14

So, the maximum value of the expression is 2.

36) Choice C is correct

The total number of handballs in the container is $6 + 5 + 8 + 10 = 29$. Since there are 6 green handballs, the probability of selecting a green handball is $\frac{6}{29}$.

37) Choice D is correct

If Emma answered 9 out of 45 questions incorrectly, then she answered 36 questions correctly. $\frac{36}{45} \times 100 = 80\%$

38) Choice C is correct

Let x be the number. Write the equation and solve for x.

30% of $x = 12 \Rightarrow 0.30x = 12 \Rightarrow x = 12 \div 0.30 = 40$

39) Choice A is correct

Let y be Anna's age: $5y + 3 = x \rightarrow 5y = x - 3 \rightarrow y = \frac{x-3}{5}$

40) Choice B is correct

The area of a trapezoid can be determined using the formula: $A = \frac{1}{2} \times (a + b) \times h$

We know: $DC = 4\ cm$, $AE = 2\ cm$, and $AD = 4\ cm \rightarrow$

$A = \frac{1}{2} \times (4\ cm + 2\ cm) \times 4\ cm = 12\ cm^2$

41) Choice E is correct

From the choices provided, only 0.061 is between 0.0048 and 0.069.

42) Choice C is correct

The reciprocal of $\frac{3}{5}$ is added to the reciprocal of $\frac{1}{4}$:

$\frac{4}{1} + \frac{5}{3} = \frac{12}{3} + \frac{5}{3} = \frac{17}{3}$. The reciprocal of this sum is $\frac{3}{17}$.

43) Choice D is correct

To eliminate the decimals in this equation, multiply the numerators and denominators by 100:

$$\left(\frac{0.02}{0.25}\right)\left(\frac{100}{100}\right) = \left(\frac{1.25}{x}\right)\left(\frac{100}{100}\right) \rightarrow \left(\frac{2}{25}\right) = \frac{125}{100x} \rightarrow x = \left(\frac{125}{100}\right)\left(\frac{25}{2}\right) = 15.625$$

44) Choice D is correct

From the choices provided, number -0.0028 is greater than 0.0029

45) Choice D is correct

1 pound $= 16$ ounces

1 pan $= (3 \times 16) + 8 = 56$ ounces. Now, convert ounces to pounds:

$56 \div 16 = 3.5$ pounds. Then: 5 pans $= (5 \times 3.5) = 17.5$ pounds

17.5 pounds $= 17$ pounds and $(0.5 \times 16) = 8$ ounces

46) Choice E is correct

According to the chart, grade 5 has the least number of girl students.

Grade 1 : 16 boys, 18 girls

Grade 2 : 14 boys, 16 girls

Grade 3 : 20 boys, 18 girls

Grade 4 : 17 boys, 20 girls

Grade 5 : 18 boys, 14 girls

47) Choice A is correct

Use the percent increase expression to find the answer:

$$Percent\ change = \frac{New\ Value - Old\ Value}{Old\ Value} \times 100\% \Rightarrow \frac{400 - 250}{250} \times 100\% = 60\%$$

48) Choice C is correct

Between 1990 and 2000, the number of car sales increased by 40,000 ($100,000 - 60,000$).

49) Choice D is correct

To find the $200,000 + 500,000 + 250,000 + 150,000 = 1,100,000$

50) Choice E is correct

SUV revenue in 2000: $\quad \$850,000 \times \frac{16}{100} = \frac{1,360,000}{100} = \$136,000$

SUV revenue in 2006: $\quad 980,000 \times \frac{20}{100} = \frac{1,960,000}{100} = \$196,000$

$\$196,000 - \$136,000 = \$60,000$

... So Much More Online!

Effortless Math Online CBEST Math Center offers a complete study program, including the following:

✓ Step-by-step instructions on how to prepare for the CBEST Math test

✓ Numerous CBEST Math worksheets to help you measure your math skills

✓ Complete list of CBEST Math formulas

✓ Video lessons for CBEST Math topics

✓ Full-length CBEST Math practice tests

✓ And much more...

No Registration Required.

Receive the PDF version of this book or get another FREE book!

Thank you for using our Book!

Do you LOVE this book?

Then, you can get the PDF version of this book or another book absolutely FREE!

Please email us at:

info@EffortlessMath.com

Author's Final Note

I hope you enjoyed reading this book. You've made it through the book! Great job!

First of all, thank you for purchasing this practice book. I know you could have picked any number of books to help you prepare for your CBEST Math test, but you picked this book and for that I am extremely grateful.

It took me years to write this practice book for the CBEST Math because I wanted to prepare a comprehensive CBEST Math book to help test takers make the most effective use of their valuable time while preparing for the test.

After teaching and tutoring math courses for over a decade, I've gathered my personal notes and lessons to develop this practice test. It is my greatest hope that the practice tests in this book could help you prepare for your test successfully.

If you have any questions, please contact me at reza@effortlessmath.com and I will be glad to assist. Your feedback will help me to greatly improve the quality of my books in the future and make this book even better. Furthermore, I expect that I have made a few minor errors somewhere in this book. If you think this to be the case, please let me know so I can fix the issue as soon as possible.

If you enjoyed this book and found some benefit in reading this, I'd like to hear from you and hope that you could take a quick minute to post a review on the book's Amazon page. To leave your valuable feedback, please visit: amzn.to/2TcbwOr

Or scan this QR code.

I personally go over every single review, to make sure my books really are reaching out and helping students and test takers. Please help me help CBEST Math test takers, by leaving a review!

I wish you all the best in your future success!

Reza Nazari

Math teacher and author